Micro Analysis of Bajaj Auto Limited(Two Wheeler)

:: Author ::

Prakash Parmar
(M.Com., B.ed.,NET., M.B.A)

PUBLISHED BY

Hemchandracharya International Publishing House
HQ. At & Po. Chaveli., Ta- Chansma,
Dist- Patan, North Gujarat, India, Asia.
www.iphouseindia.com

First Publication: 6TH JANURUARY, 2015

Copyright: Author

(c) **Prakash Parmar**

ISBN:- 978-15-08675-66-2

Price: Rs.800/- INDIA

    $ 15 OUTSIDE INDIA

PUBLISHED BY

Hemchandracharya International Publishing House
HQ. At & Po. Chaveli., Ta- Chansma,
Dist- Patan, North Gujarat, India, Asia.
www.iphouseindia.com

Dedicated to
my
Loving
Son
Vraj

INDEX

AUTOMOBILE INDUSTRY IN INDIA

Indian automobile industry in India is as well developed as any top industrial nations. Long years of License Raj and protectionism led to the development of various segments of automobile industry. There are a large number of well-entered players in all segments of the automobile industry as depicted in the following table.

Graph 1:

DIFFERENT SEGMENT OF AUTOMOBILE INDUSTRY IN INDIA

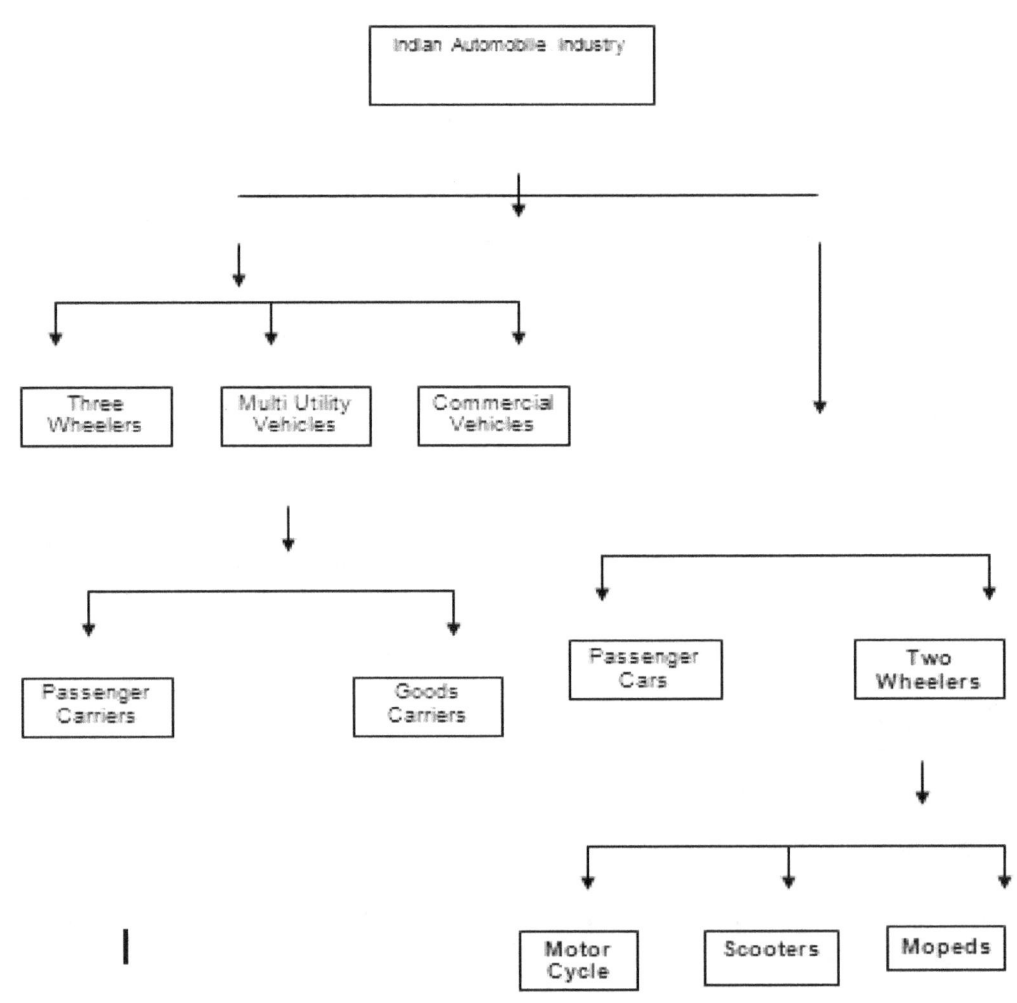

There are also exists a huge market and production base for specialty vehicles like Tractors, Earthmoving vehicles, Cranes etc. But despite having a well-developed industry and a large market, the industry still has not been able to realize its full potential owing to the following reasons.

- Low purchasing power
- Price sensitive market
- Existence of a large middle class
- Insufficient transportation infrastructure

India as a country has a per capita income of around US$797 per annum. That is very low as compared with the developed nations like Japan or the USA, which is in the range of $20000. Though there is a existence of a large middle class, majority of them in the lower end ensures that the disposable income left with the masses is comparatively less. Hence the possession of an automobile is considered a luxury and often avoided by people.

But the scenario is after all not that bad and the industry as a whole is growing in terms of volume although the profitability and profit margin is of question.

Table: 1

Market shares of different segment in india

Domestic Market Share for 2007-08

CVs	5.05%
Total Passenger Vehicles	16.4%
Total Two Wheelers	75.13%
Three Wheelers	3.78%

(source: ACMA 2007-08)

(source:www.siamindia.com/scripts/market share.dspx.)

Graph:2

Category-Wise Market Share in 2007-08

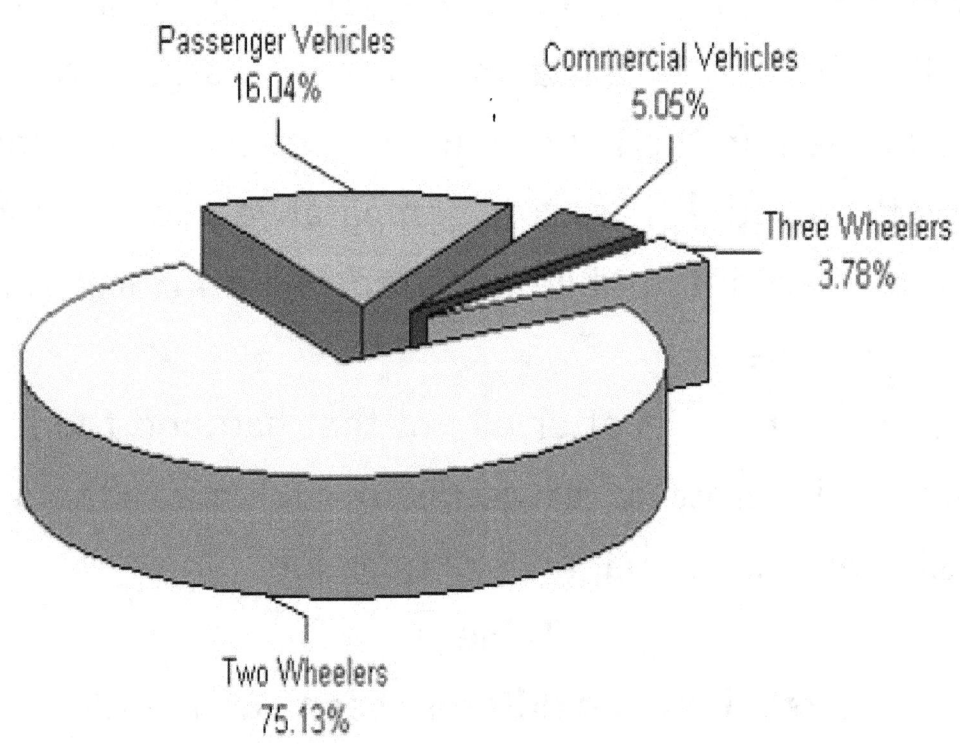

This graph shows the segmentation of Indian Automobile Industry. There are mainly four segments Two wheeler, Three wheeler, Passenger vehicles, Commercial vehicles. As per the graph Two wheeler has the highest market share that is 75.13%, and the commercial vehicles has the lowest one that is 5.05%. The two wheeler industry is about to witness a shift in dynamics with new breed of bikes hitting the market. This spells though times for exiting two wheeler majors. Honda's 'Unicorn', the 150cc motorcycle for the premium segment, is the first among the many new range of bikes scheduled to excite customers.

Table : 2

MARKET SHARES OF VARIOUS FIRMS:

Market Share of Key Players in 2006-07	
Hero Honda Motors	42%
Bajaj Auto Ltd.	27%
TVS Motor Co.	19%
HMSIL	9%
Others	3%

Source: SIAM, IMaCS Analysis

Source:www.siamindia.com/script/marketshare.

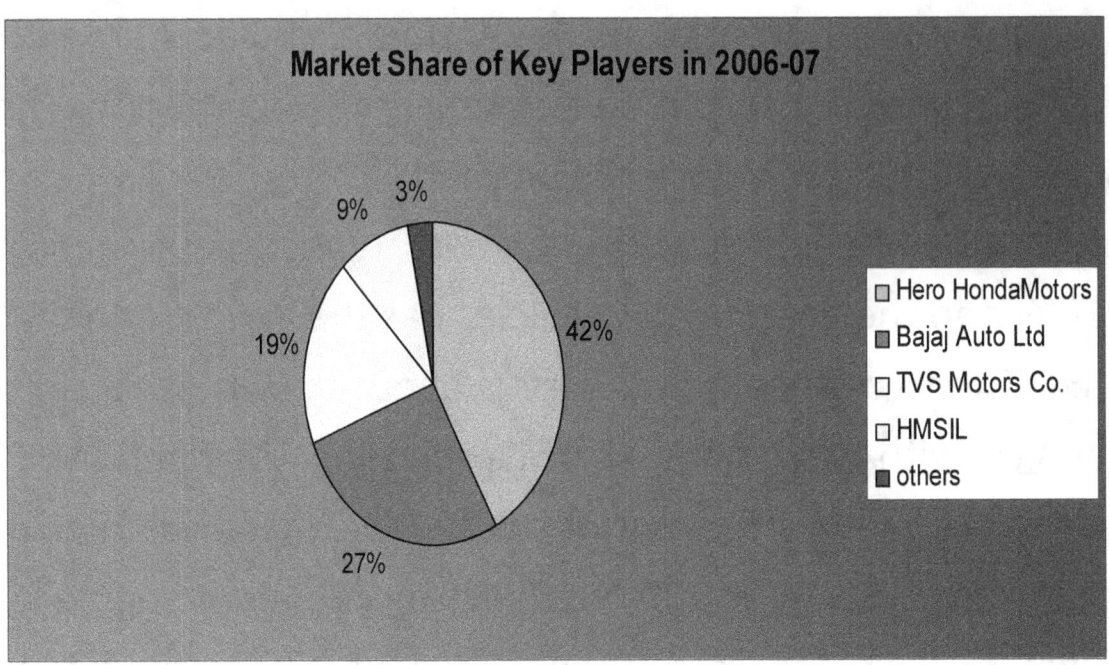

In the Indian two wheeler market, competition is intense with around 10 players competing for the share in the industry. These players include global giants like Honda, Suzuki and Yamaha as well as Indian players like Bajaj and TVS. The market leader in the domestic two wheeler industry is Hero Honda Motors, with a 42 % market share. It is the largest two wheeler manufacturer in the world and is closely followed by Bajaj Auto, which has a 27 % market share. TVS Motor is the third largest two wheeler manufacturer in the country, it has also established a manufacturing facility in Indonesia. Honda Motors is present in India as Honda Motorcycles and Scooters India Limited (HMSIL), a 100 % subsidiary, in addition to its joint venture, Hero Honda. Another international player, Suzuki, has recently entered the Indian market through its direct subsidiary. The industry is characterized by frequent product launches, with over 20 models launched in 200

THE BAJAJ AUTO LIMITED

History

Bajaj Auto came into existence on November 29, 1945 as M/s Bachraj Trading Corporation Private Limited. It started off by selling imported two- and three-wheelers in India. In 1959, it obtained license from the Government of India to manufacture two- and three-wheelers and it went public in 1960. In 1970, it rolled out its 100,000th vehicle. In 1977, it managed to produce and sell 100,000 vehicles in a single financial year. In 1985, it started producing at Waluj in Aurangabad. In 1986, it managed to produce and sell 500,000 vehicles in a single financial year. In 1995, it rolled out its ten millionth vehicle and produced and sold 1 million vehicles in a year.

According to the authors of *Globality: Competing with Everyone from Everywhere for Everything.* Bajaj has grown operations in 50 countries by creating a line of value-for-money bikes targeted to the different preferences of entry-level buyers with quality such that Kawasaki buys Bajaj products for some of its markets.

Bajaj Auto Ltd (BAL) is the second largest two wheeler market in India. It was established in 1945, as a trading company and obtained a production license in 1959. it initially struck a technical collaboration with piaggio of Itlaly but later started selling products under the Bajaj brand name.

Unit Profile :

Bajaj auto limited, Waluj, Aurangabad, is a division of Bajaj Auto Limited, Pune, a flagship company of Bajaj Group. Bajaj Group was formed by Mr. Jamanalal Bajaj in 1929. Bajaj Auto Limited, Pune started scooter production in 1960. As an expansion plan, Bajaj Auto Limited, Waluj Plant is started in 1985. In 1999, a State of Art Plant was started at Chakan.

Objectives of Bajaj Auto Limited are to cater the market needs of transportation by providing 2 wheeler and 3 wheeler vehicles. BALW has been producing the catalogue products to cater to the changing market requirements. Based on the customer feedback, improvements are being made continuously in the existing products. In the process of introducing new products, emission requirements are being taken into consideration and products manufactured are meeting the regulatory requirements.

Pantnagar, April 9, 2007: Bajaj Auto Limited today inaugurated its Greenfield Plant with a planned capacity of one million motorcycles per annum at Pantnagar, Uttarakhand. Built on a total area of 65 acres with the balance 155 acres allocated to the vendor cluster, the Pantnagar facility would be Bajaj Auto's fourth Plant & first Plant outside Maharashtra. The unit has a plant area of 40,000 sq mtr and will employ 600 line engineers who have been trained at Chakan for 3 months.

Amongst the motorcycles being considered for India launch, recently redesigned Kawasaki Ninja 250 is amongst the front runner. The 250cc liquid cool baby ninja develops an impressive 30ps at 10500rpm. Apart from that, ER-6n, Ninja ZX-6R, Z1000 and Vulcan are likely to be released in India through Bajaj Pro-Biking showrooms.

Spinoffs and Acquisitions

It has been reported that Bajaj is headed for a de-merger into two separate companies: Bajaj Auto and Bajaj Finance. It is expected that the sum of the parts created will be worth more that the current whole, as was the case in the de-merger of Reliance Industries.

In November 2007, Bajaj Auto acquired 14.5% stake in KTM Power Sports AG (holding company of KTM Sportmotocycles AG). The two companies have signed a cooperation deal, by which KTM will provide the know-how for joint development of the water-cooled 4 stroke 125 and 250 cc engines, and Bajaj will take over the distribution of KTM products in India and some other Southeast Asian nations. Bajaj Auto said it is open to take a majority stake in KTM and is also looking at other takeover opportunities. On the 8th of January 2008, Managing Director Rajiv Bajaj confirmed the collaboration and announced Bajaj Auto's intention to gradually increase their stake in KTM to 25%

Low cost cars

Bajaj Auto says its $2,500 car, which it is building with Renault and Nissan Motor, will aim at a fuel-efficiency of 30 km/litre, or twice an average small car, and carbon dioxide emissions of 100 gm/km.

It is a Tata Nano competitor. The Bajaj venture will have an initial capacity of 400,000 units, while Tata expects eventual demand of 1 million Nanos.

Timeline of new releases

- 1960-1970 - Vespa 150 - Under the licence of Piaggio of Italy
- 1971 - three-wheeler goods carrier
- 1972 - Bajaj Chetak
  - 1976 - Bajaj Super
- 1977 - Rear engine Autorickshaw
- 1981 - Bajaj M-50
- 1986 - Bajaj M-80, Kawasaki Bajaj KB100
- 1990 - Bajaj Sunny
- 1991 - Kawasaki Bajaj 4S Champion
- 1994 - Bajaj Classic
- 1995 - Bajaj Super Excel

- 1997 - Kawasaki Bajaj Boxer, Rear Engine Diesel Autorickshaw
- 1998 - Kawasaki Bajaj Caliber, Bajaj Legend, India's first four-stroke scooter, Bajaj Spirit
- 2000 - <u>Bajaj Saffire</u>
- 2001 - <u>Eliminator</u>, <u>Bajaj Pulsar</u>
- 2003 - Caliber115, Bajaj Wind 125, <u>Bajaj Pulsar</u>
- 2004 - <u>Bajaj CT 100</u>, New Bajaj Chetak 4-stroke with Wonder Gear, Bajaj Discover DTS-i
- 2005 - <u>Bajaj Wave</u>, <u>Bajaj Avenger</u>, <u>Bajaj Discover</u>
- 2006 - <u>Bajaj Platina</u>
- 2007 - Bajaj Pulsar-200(Oil Cooled), Bajaj Kristal,<u>Bajaj Pulsar 220 DTS-Fi(Fuel Injection)</u> , <u>XCD 125 DTS-Si (Pronounced Exceed 125 DTS-Si)</u>
- 2008 - Bajaj Discover 135 DTS-i - sport (Upgrade of existing 135 model)

Bajaj to launch six new motorcycles in 2009

To counter the slowdown, Bajaj Auto today announced slew of incentives. The measures include an intense new product initiatives. Through this measure, Bajaj will launch a new motorcycle each month for 6 months beginning January 2009. The new motorcycles we can expect from the Bajaj includes - **new face lifted Pulsar 220cc, new Pulsar 200 FI, XCD sprint, Blade scooter,** new low cost product (might be called as

Steel) and an unknown product. Seems like Bajaj will fire on all cylinders in 2009...

COMPANY'S PHILOSOPHY & BELIEF'S

- ➢ We approach our responsibilities with ambition and resourcefulness.
- ➢ We organize ourselves for a transparent and harmonious flow of work.
- ➢ We respect sound theory and encourage creative experimentation.
- ➢ And we make our workplace a source of pride.
- ➢ Transparency – a commitment that the business is managed along transparent lines.
- ➢ Fairness – to all stakeholders in the Company, but especially to minority shareholders.
- ➢ Disclosure – of all relevant financial and non financial information in an easily understood manner.
- ➢ Supervision – of the company's activities by a professionally competent and independent management and board of directors.

MANAGEMENT PROFILE

Rahul Bajaj	Chairman
Madhur Bajaj	Vice Chairman
Rajiv Bajaj	Managing Director

Sanjiv Bajaj	Executive Director
Abraham Joseph	Vice President (Research & Development)
Pradeep Shrivastava	President (Engineering)
S Sridhar	CEO (2WH)
R C Maheshwari	CEO (Commercial Vehicles)
Rakesh Sharma	CEO (International Business)
C P Tripathi	Vice President (Corporate)
N H Hingorani	Vice President (Commercial)
Kevin P D'sa	Vice President (Finance)
S Ravikumar	Vice President (Business Development)
K Srinivas	Vice President (Human Resources)
J. Sridhar	Company Secretary

Jankidevi Bajaj Gram Vikas Sanstha (JBGVS)
Bajaj Auto's Corporate Social Responsibility towards the rural poor is carried out by a trust, Jankidevi Bajaj Gram Vikas Sanstha (JBGVS). This trust was formed in 1987. JBGVS acts as a catalyst for development at the grass root level in 44 villages around Bajaj Auto plants in Pune and Aurangabad District.

Vision Statement of JBGV

JBGVS, a Registered Society and a Trust, is an apolitical and secular organisation which aims to act as a catalyst for rural and urban development. It assists the resident community of the selected villages and areas, in integrated development, making their villages and areas into models of excellence for others to emulate.

Organizational Overview of Rural Development

JBGVS will work with the participating rural community in the selected villages to improve their quality of life. Stress is laid on alleviation of poverty, health care, education, empowerment of women & gender justice. We strive to motivate our rural community to willingly and enthusiastically undertake the improvement of their villages, so that they become models of excellence within 5 to 7 years.

Implementation strategy

(1) To ensure the involvement of our rural community, JBGVS relies on a participatory approach in implementing all its projects.

(2) In addition, the trust secures the participation of local elected bodies like the Gram Panchayat (village council), Co-operative Societies, Self Help Groups, Women and Youth Clubs in decision making.

(3) JBGVS undertakes large-scale human resource development projects in agriculture, animal husbandry, dairy, horticulture,

health, education and income generation to accelerate the pace of development activities.

(4) JBGVS disengages from the village that achieves 80% of development as per our social indicators and discontinues active participation but monitors their progress incase they need assistance and guidance. JBGVS plan for Integrated Rural Development rolls on to another village awaiting development.

The Inevitable Change

Bajaj on internal analysis found that it lacked -

1. The technical expertise to deliver competitive goods.

2. The design know-how.

3. And the immediate inability to support the onslaught of competitors.

All these forced Bajaj to look for an international partner who could bring in technology and also offer some basic platforms to be manufactured and marketed in India. Kawasaki of Japan is a world-renowned manufacturer of high performance bikes. Bajaj entered into a strategic tie-up with Kawasaki in late 1990s to enhance its product line and knowledge up-gradation to support long-term strategies.

This served the purpose of sustaining the market competition for a while. From 1996 to 2000, Bajaj invested hugely in infrastructure while simultaneously developing product design and innovation capabilities, which is the prime reason behind the energetic Bajaj of 21st century. Bajaj introduced a slew of products right from entry-level motorcycle to the high premium segment right from 2001 onwards, and since then its raining success all the way for Bajaj.

Last quarter, Bajaj had impressive performance growing at a rate of 20%+ when the largest manufacturer grew at just 6%. This stands a testimony to the various important strategic decisions over the past decade.

PRODUCT PROFILE

products

Some of the models that Bajaj makes (or has made including prototypes) are:

Scooters Bajaj Kristal DTSi

Cars

Bajaj Lite concept

Bajaj ULC (ultra-low cost)- the Tata Nano competitor.

Motorcycles

- Bajaj CT 100
- Bajaj Platina
- Bajaj Discover 110cc
- Bajaj Discover DTS-i 125cc
- Bajaj Discover 135cc DTS-i
- Bajaj XCD 125 DTS-Si
- Bajaj Discover DTS-i 135cc

- <u>Bajaj Pulsar</u> 150 DTSi
- <u>Bajaj Pulsar</u> 180 DTSi
- <u>Bajaj Pulsar</u> 200 DTSi
- <u>Bajaj Pulsar 220 DTS-Fi</u>
- <u>Bajaj Avenger</u>

Upcoming Models

- Bajaj Sonic
- Bajaj Discover 150
- <u>Bajaj XCD 125 sprint</u>
- Bajaj Ninja

Discontinued Models

- <u>Bajaj Sunny</u>
- <u>Bajaj Chetak</u>
- <u>Bajaj Cub</u>
- Bajaj Super
- <u>Bajaj Saffire</u>
- <u>Bajaj Wave</u>
- Bajaj Legend
- Bajaj Bravo
- <u>Kawasaki Eliminator</u>
- <u>Bajaj Kawasaki Wind 125</u>
- Bajaj Kawasaki 4s Champion
- Bajaj Kawasaki KB 100 RTZ
- Bajaj Boxer

- Bajaj Caliber
- Bajaj Wind

CURRENT MODELS OF BAJAJ AUTO LTD.

Bajaj Avenger

Being the first Indian cruiser, Bajaj Avenger, developed by an Indian Company-Bajaj Auto, is among the likes of Yamaha Enticer and Kawasaki Eliminator. Built-in with DTS-i technology, this cruiser is specially designed to suit the Indian roads.Bajaj avenger is equipped with the 180 cc DTS-i engine technology that gives its rider a better riding experience. Its low-slung body coupled with a chrome texture, makes this. cruiser

 exceptionally noticeable and striking. The Bajaj Avenger features a comfy seating arrangement.Its saddle like seat gives you a very restful pleasure of riding, a backrest for pillion, frontward foot-riding stance

gives you an experience no less than riding a HarleyDavidson's

Engine

Type	4 stroke, DTS-i
Displacement	180 cc
Max Power	16.5 bhp / 12.15 @ 8000 rpm
Max Torque	15.22 Nm @ 4500 rpm

Brakes

Front Brakes	Hydraulically operated Disc Brakes-260mm
Rear Brakes	130 mm Drum
Electrical System	
System Voltage	12 V, AC
Head Lamp	60 / 55 W (Halogen)
Horn	12 V, AC

Bajaj Discover DTS-i

The 125cc Bajaj Discover has become a new market leader with the introduction of DTSi technology in the bike. The Baja Discover bike also called *Jaddoo* comes with highly developed accessories and arresting features that never fail to pull the attention of people around.

Its graphics, powerful built and the brawny structure make the bike look extremely chic. Some of the best features of the Bajaj Discover DTSi are its opt prism headlamp coupled with twin pilot lamps, twin pod console and a host of other features. For a great riding experience the Discover has been equipped with Spring and Spring (SNS) rear suspension along with triple rated springs that boasts of longest travel of 110mm, telescopic front suspension of 30mm that assures longest travel of 135mm.

Engine

Type	4 stroke, DTS-i, Natural cooled air
Displacement	124.52 cc
Max Power	8.47 kW (11.51 Ps) @8000 rpm
Max Torque	10.8 Nm @ 6500rpm
Transmission	4 - Speed constant mesh
Clutch	Wet, Multidisc type

Ignition System	Microprocessor Controlled Digital CDI
Starting System	Kick Start/ Self-Start

Bajaj Platina

The Bajaj Platina made its debut on the Indian roads in the year 2006. An imitation of the Bajaj CT-100, the Platina is again a 100 CC bike, like the Bajaj CT 100. With a better gearbox, optional alloy wheels and body structure, the Platina is a great bike. The bike boasts of bigger dimensions as compared to the CT 100, which gives its ride better stability and riding quality.

 The Platina logo and sticker on the side panels of the bike is yet another striking feature of this wonderful Bajaj bike.

Bajaj Kristal DTSi has been acclaimed highly by the automobile critics and columnists as first among the scooters in India with facilities like front fuelling capability, side stand alarm, automatic lamp characteristics and extra battery life as compared to other scooters of the same category. Its extra large fuel tank is capable of storing about 4.5 liters of petrol on an approximate basis and has a maximum speed capacity of 120km/hr.

Engine

Type	4 stroke
Cooling Type	Natural Air Cooled

Fuel Tank

Fuel Tank Capacity	13.0 L (Reserve: 2 L)

Bajaj Pulsar DTSi

The innovation of Pulsar DTS-i by Bajaj was a revolution in its own right. The first version of the Pulsar bike itself was a huge success. With its masculine and hardy body structure, the Pulsar was a massive hit among the die-hard biker fans. And then came the *all-new Pulsar* with an in-built DTS-i technology.

The new look of Pulsar DTS-I although is very much similar to its first edition but the new version carries an élan with it. Power-packed with a host of new-fangled technologies, the DTS-i Pulsar has embarked on new the system of *digital biking* in India. Apart from the DTS-i this new Pulsar also has TRICS III and digital CDI technology incorporated in it.

Parameter	Pulsar 180 DTS-i	Pulsar 150 DTS-i
Engine Response	New silencer with ExhausTEC technology now ensures Improved engine torque even at varying load conditions	

tyres	Broader 100/90 rear tyres as standard on both variants

Bajaj Wave

The Bajaj Wave is a 100 cc scooter from the house of Bajaj Auto. Its 4-stroke engine delivers 8 bhp (5.88 Kw) of power and a torque of 0.9 kgm. With its well-sophisticated DTSi technologically designed engine coupled with ExhausTEC offers far super performance and riding experience than other of its kind.

The streamlined, sleek body structure along with twofold color tone gives this scooter an ultra modern look. The body design of the Bajaj Wave is such that parking is never a problem for the owners of this wonderful scooter.

The seating arrangements and a spacious storage prove very handy. The Bajaj Wave comes in the following colors that are mentioned below:

- Beige
- Metallic Black
- Purple and
- Red

Engine

Type	Single Cylinder, 4 stroke
Displacement	109.7 cc
Max. Power	8.0 BHP @ 7000 RPM (5.88 KW)

Max. Torque	0.9 Kgm @ 5000 RPM
Starting Mechanism	KICK AND ELECTRIC START

Bajaj XCD 125 Sprint

Bajaj has once again struck the right cords with several middle class consumers with its new launch. The all new Bajaj XCD 125 Sprint bike is set to sweep the hearts of several consumers. It is equipped with all the latest features and is certainly a dream bike.

It suits the requirements of any bike lover who is looking forward to fuel efficiency and at the same time style and elegance. The bike has a 125 digital Speak swirl Induction Engine and XCD technology with delivers an amazing output. Take a look at the model's technical specifications to see just how good it is.

The Bajaj XCD 125 Sprint has been road tested to check its mileage and performance and has been done so with success and good feedback

Engine	
Model Designation	Digital Twin Spark - Swirl

	induction (DTS-SI)
No. Of Cylinders	4
Type	Four stroke Natural Air-cooled
Clutch	Multi-Plate Wet type
Displacement (cc)	124.58 cc
Ignition system	Microprocessor controlled Digital CDI, with TRICS incorporated in Carburettor Ignition Timing
Gear Box	04 Gear Constant Mesh
Suspension	
Front	Telescopic (125 mm travel)

Bajaj Kristal DTS- i

The Bajaj Kristal DTS-i is the second vehicle in the scooterette segment to be launched by Bajaj Auto. It is targeted at the young college girls and is designed for easy city riding. The Bajaj Kristal DTS-i proves to be an ideal city scooter especially for young women who wish to travel city distances daily.

The Kristal DTS-i boasts of the Bajaj patented **Digital Twin Spark Ignition (DTS-i)** technology with **ExhausTEC** which offers excellent driving capabilities. Kristal DTS-Iis fitted with a 95cc engine which delivers a power of 7.2 Ps (5.38 KW) at 7,500 rpm, the maximum torque of this bike is around 7.66 Nm at 5,500 rpm.

This vehicle is also armed with the revolutionary **Spring-in-Suspension technology (SNS)** for a comfortable experience. Provision of storage space of 22 liters below the comfortable seat, allows the rider to have a comfortable ride and store things which are shopped during the trip as well. The single key performs many function such as opening up the accelerator lock, steering seat lock and ignition as well.

It has the unique Front Fueling system that ensures a convenient refueling for the rider. The fuel tank opens up with the ignition key too. The capacity of the fuel tank is 6 liters while the mileage stands at 50km/l.

The Bajaj Kristal DTS-i is designed keeping in mind the practicality in use and comfort of the rider. This light weight and gearless scooter weighs 100 kg only is easy to operate.

Vital Accessories of the Bajaj Krista DTS-i

- Fuel Gauge,
- Analog
- Distance counter
- Indicators for the side stand,
- Turn Lights& High Beam.

The Bajaj Kristal DTS-i is quite easy to handle and is available in attractive colors such as silver, black, blue and read. The newest entrant from the Bajaj stable is a style statement for the young college going girls and young working women as well.

Engine :	Four-stroke/petrol
Transmission :	Four-speed
Engine Displacement :	100 cc
Tachometer :	No
Max Power :	22b hp@5400 rpm
Wheel base :	1,370mm
Clearance :	140mm
Ignition :	Coil ignition
Dry Weight :	163kg
Fuel tank Capacity :	14.5itres
Battery :	12V

FUNCTIONAL AREAS
MARKETING

As a strategy, the company is segregating rural market from urban.

In the first phase, it will be sitting up 20 outlets in affluent, but severely under penetrated, rural districts, by March 2007. Special schemes and financial products suited for the rural market will be launched. Bajaj's non-banking financial arm, Bajaj Auto Financial Ltd (BAFL), is expected to play a key role here.

The strategy of having exclusive rural dealers has met with reasonable of success. In Nashik, the company earlier has two outlets, both in the city, and barely a kilometer away from each other. It closed down one, and opened another one 35 km away fro the city. Resulting both outlets are catering to exclusive catchments area and are closer to their customers. A rural customers no longer needs to travels to the city to buy or service his two-wheeler.

And Bajaj is taking the classical marketing route to enter the rural mind space. They will train the sons and daughter o village VIPs, who are also the opinion makers and thought leaders of their respective villages, to do this. The company expects its rural outlets to achieve a breakeven at 175-200 vehicles a month. It estimated the cost of setting up rural outlets at Rs. 40 lacs, with working capital requirement of Rs. 2 crores. Catering to a large number of 'unbankable' customers in rural India is a challenge.

The focus of BAL off late has been on providing the best of the class models at competitive prices. Most of the Bajaj models come loaded with the latest features within the price band acceptable by the market. BAL has been the pioneer in stretching competition into providing latest features in the price segment by updating the low price bikes with the latest features like disk-brakes, anti-skid technology and dual suspension, etc.

Bajaj auto had done the journey from the "Hamara Bajaj to distinctly ahead" because of the drastic declining in the sale of the CHETAK in 1990. The sales was declining because of the change in the consumer preference form riding scooters to 4-stroke engine motor cycle.

Reoriented business launched series of new motorcycle in Market. And change in the communication strategy from:-

Graph : 3

```
┌──────────────────────────┐
│      HAMARA BAJAJ        │
└──────────────────────────┘
              │
              ▼
┌──────────────────────────┐
│   INSPIRING CONFIDENCE   │
└──────────────────────────┘
```

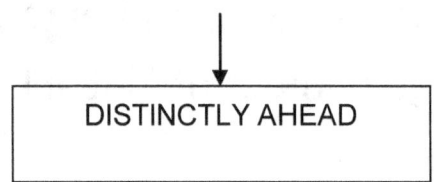

DISTINCTLY AHEAD

From the year, 2007 the company applies the communication strategy of the Distinctly ahead from the Inspiring Confidence. It focuses on the 3 core values of Innovaton, Speed and perfection.

Starting from its inception, BAL adopted different marketing strategies for different models, few of them are discussed below: -

Kawasaki 4S - First attempt by Bajaj to make a mark in the motorcycle segment. The target customer was the father in the family but the target audience of the commercial was the son in the family. The time at which Kawasaki 4S was launched Hero Honda was the market leader in fuel-efficient bikes and Yamaha in the performance bikes.

The commercial of Kawasaki 4S had the punch line "Kyun Hero" means "now what hero" which reflected the aggressiveness in the marketing front by the company.

Boxer - It took the reins from where the Kawasaki 4S left. Target was the rural population and the price sensitive customer. Boxer marketed as a value for money bike with great mileage. Larger wheelbase, high ground clearance and high mileage were the selling factors and it was in direct competition to Hero Honda Dawn and Suzuki MX100.

Caliber - The focus for the Caliber 115 was youth. And though Bajaj made the bike look bigger and feel more powerful than its predecessor (characteristics that will attract the average, 25-plus, executive segment bike buyer), its approach towards advertising is even more radically different this time around. Bajaj gave the mandate for the ad campaign to Lowe, picking them from the clique of three agencies that do promos for the company (the other two being Leo Burnett and O&M). Going by the initial market response, the campaign was clearly a hit in the 5-10 years age bracket. So, the teaser campaign and the emphasis on the Caliber 115 being a *`Hoodibabaa'* bike placed it as a trendy motorcycle for the college-goers and the 25 plus executives both at the same time.

Pulsar - Pulsar was launched in direct competition to the Hero Honda's 'CBZ' model in 150 cc plus segment. The campaign beared innovative punch line of "Definitely Male" positioning Pulsar to be a masculine-looking model with an appeal to the performance sensitive customers. The Pulsar went one step ahead of Hero Honda's 'CBZ' and launched a twin variant of Pulsar with the 180 cc model. The model was a great success and has already crossed 1 million mark in sales.

Discover - The same DTSI technology of Pulsar extended to 125 cc Discover was a great success. With this, Bajaj could realize its success riding on the back of technological innovation rather than the joint venture way followed by competitors to gain market share.

Strategies for the Overseas Markets

Bajaj Auto looks at external markets primarily with three strategies: -

1) A market where all BAL need to do is distribute through CKD or CBU routes.

2) Markets where BAL need to create new products.

3) Markets where BAL need to enter with existing products and probably with a good distributor or a production facility or a joint venture.

Earlier, most of the products that Bajaj exported were scooters and some motorcycles. However, in its target markets, like in India, the shift was towards motorcycles. With the expansion in Bajaj's own range to almost five-six platforms of motorcycles, it had a better offering to export, also the reason for its stronger showing. For the last fiscal, 60 per cent of its exports were two-wheelers and the rest three-wheelers. Of the two-wheeler exports, close to 90 per cent were motorcycles.

Bajaj has identified certain key markets, which hold potential. Its first overseas office established at the Jebel Ali free trade zone has been the focal point for exports to middle Africa and the Saharan nations. Egypt and Iran also continue to be strong markets for Bajaj.

The other market, which would be a focus area, is South America, where the company feels it is fairly well represented in most countries, except in Brazil, the largest market. The company recently participated in a large auto exhibition in Brazil and found good consumer acceptance to products like Pulsar and Wind 125.

The other focus area is the ASEAN nations, which constitute the third biggest consumer of two-wheelers. The biggest among them is Indonesia, where Bajaj distributors are looking to introduce eco-friendly four-stroke auto rickshaws. But two-wheeler market requires great deal of effort from BAL. Everybody is there with Honda leading the show. There's Suzuki, Kawasaki and some Korean and Chinese models. BAL should look at the right product mix for two-wheelers. Bajaj's Pulsar model has taken off well there. It also wants to develop a new step-through model for the Indonesian market, but for now it will create a base there with its motorcycle models.

Bajaj has also made a beginning by selling bikes in the Philippines branded in the name of its technical partner, Kawasaki. The two signed an MoU in February. Kawasaki, a large multi-product conglomerate, only makes high-end bikes and does not have sub-200cc models. Kawasaki is marketing the new model, Wind 125, developed by both companies, in the Philippines. The Bajaj-developed models, Caliber and Byk, which is a fuel-efficient bike, are also being distributed by Kawasaki. This is a good beginning strategically for Kawasaki to evince interest in Bajaj products for markets which can still buy less than 150 cc.

BAL is also all set to increase its share in the domestic market with a tie-up with banking major State Bank of India through which it hopes to leverage the latter's nine thousand strong branch networks to offer two wheeler loans at affordable rates to customers.

In additions to giving a whole new segment of populace across the country easy to finance for buying two-wheelers, we are also betting that it will aspiration buying and upgrading within our existing consumer base. While 24 percent of the company's two wheeler sales currently comes from finance extended by Bajaj Auto Finance ltd and ICICI, the company is hoping that the bank's network grow sales significantly in smaller towns where finance is currently offers by the unorganized sector from rates varying between 18-24 percent as against the 10.5 per cent for three years that SBI will offer

Graph : 4

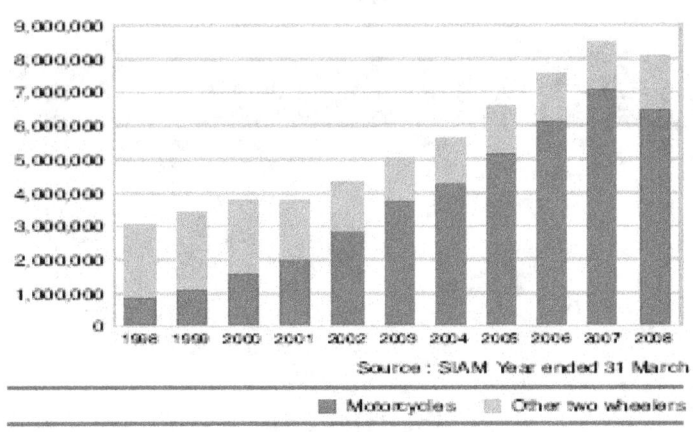

Industry's sale of Two-Wheelers

Source : SIAM Year ended 31 March

■ Motorcycles ■ Other two wheelers

(In Volume)

As per the chart we shows that there are continues increases in the sales of Motorcycles. But in the year from 2007 to 2008 it decreases up to some level. The decade from 1997-98 to 2006-07 was spectacular for India's two-wheeler industry. It saw impressive year-on-year growth in domestic demand for two-wheelers, driven by the sales of motorcycles. Here are the facts. In terms of volumes, the compounded annual growth rate (CAGR) of two-wheeler sales between 1997-98 and 2006-07 was 12%; and for motorcycles, it was a staggering 25.6%. This phenomenal decade of growth was abruptly, albeit temporarily, halted in 2007-08. From 8.47 million in 2006-07, overall two-wheelers sale fell by 4.8% to 8.07 million in 2007-08. The decline in motorcycle sales was sharper: by 7.8%, from 7.1 million vehicles sold in 2006-07 to 6.54 million in 2007⊠08. Chart A gives the data.

Motorcycle sales – industry and Bajaj auto
Table : 3

Year ended 31 March	Market (nos.)	Market growth	BAL (nos.)	BAL's growth	BAL's market share
2003	3,757,125	31.3%	868,138	32.3%	23.1%
2004	4,316,777	14.9%	1,023,551	17.9%	23.7%
2005	5,217,996	20.9%	1,449,710	41.6%	27.8%
2006	6,200,749	18.8%	1,912,306	31.9%	30.8%
2007	7,099,551	14.5%	2,379,499	24.4%	33.5%
2008	6,544,482	-7.8%	2,139,779	-10.1%	32.7%

Graph : 5
The Market Segment for Motorcycles

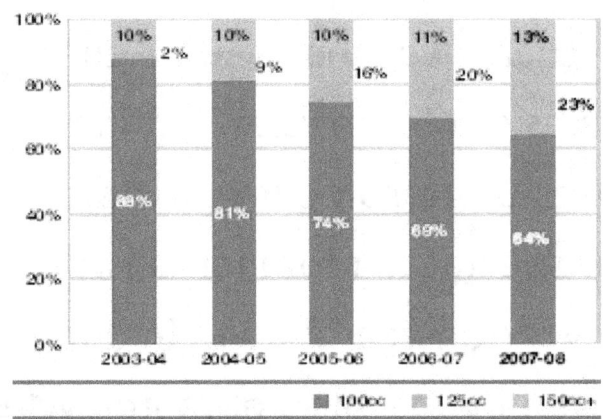

1. T he high performance segment: This includes motorcycles in the engine class of 150 cc and above. Bajaj Auto is present here with the Pulsar range (150 cc, 180 cc, 200 cc and the new 220 cc) and the Avenger DTS-i.

2. T he 125 cc segment: Bajaj Auto is in this category with the upgraded Discover

DTS-i 135 and, more significantly, the XCD 125 DTS-Si, which was launched in

September 2007.

3. T he 100 cc segment: Here, Bajaj Auto offers the Platina.

Without doubt, the market is moving towards the 125 cc and above segment, with an increasing mass migrating to the 125 cc variants. In fact, Bajaj Auto has catalysed this trend, and it forms the core of the Company's integrated marketing, product development and R&D strategy. Chart B shows the trend—where the 125 cc market has grown from 2% of total motorcycle sales in 2003□04 to 23% in 2007-08, and the 150 cc plus market has grown from 10% to 13% over the same period. The chart also shows the sharply falling share of the 100 cc entry segment, from 88% of the market in 2003-04 to 64% in 2007-08.

FINANCE

Bajaj Auto Ltd, from January to March 2007 had witnessed the beginnings of slackening domestic demand for two-wheelers "because of the sharp tightening of non-food credit by the Reserve Bank of India and all commercial banks and non-banking financing companies". Banks and finance companies significantly reduced their exposure to auto loans, and severely curtailed the supply of credit .the twin effects of higher interests and lower very badly.

Thus, after a decade of spectacular double-digit growth, two-wheelers suddenly faced a slump. For the first time in over 10 years, the industry as a whole witnessed negative growth. From 8.47 million in 2006-07, overall two-wheelers sales fell by 4.8% to 8.07 million in 2007-08. the decline in motorcycle sales was sharper still: by 7.8%, from 7. million vehicles sold in 2006-07 to 6.54 million in 2007-08.

Bajaj Auto Ltd. has been affected by this downturn. Falling demand coupled with sharply rising cost of critical raw material such as steel, especially in the second half of 2007-08, has affected both sales and profits. Given below are the key results:

➤ Despite an impressive growth in exports, Bajaj Auto's motorcycle sales by volume fell by 0% over the previous year, to 2. 4 million vehicles in 2007-08. Thus, your company's net sales fell by 6.8% to Rs.86.63 billion.

➤ Operating EBITDA (earnings before interest, taxes, depreciation and amortization) fell by 9.6% to Rs. 2.94 billion in 2007-08. This translated to an operating EBITDA margin of 4.3% of operating income, compared to 5% in the previous year.

➤ Operating profit before tax (PBT) fell by 6.7% to Rs. 0.2 billion in 2007-08. Two wheeler manufacturer in India. Bajaj Auto struggle with rapidly declining sales of Scooters, even as it was trying to make its mark in motorcycles.

Graph : 6

DUPONT CHART

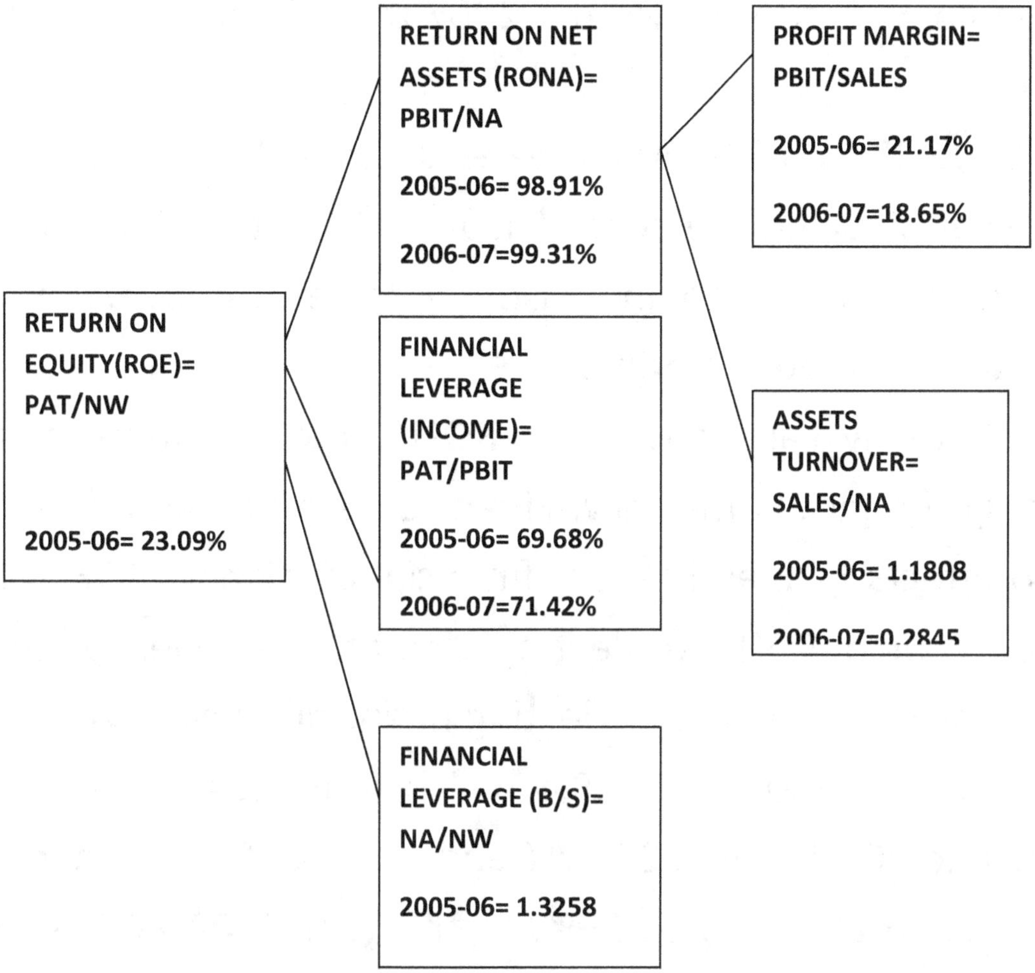

RETURN ON NET ASSETS (RONA)= PBIT/NA 2005-06= 98.91% 2006-07=99.31%	PROFIT MARGIN= PBIT/SALES 2005-06= 21.17% 2006-07=18.65%

RETURN ON EQUITY(ROE)= PAT/NW

2005-06= 23.09%

FINANCIAL LEVERAGE (INCOME)= PAT/PBIT

2005-06= 69.68%

2006-07=71.42%

ASSETS TURNOVER= SALES/NA

2005-06= 1.1808

2006-07=0.2845

FINANCIAL LEVERAGE (B/S)= NA/NW

2005-06= 1.3258

Du pont analysis helps in the knowing the factors affecting the Return on Investment by decomposing the ROI. Assets turnover ratio focus on the relationship between sales and assets. By managing efficiently, the sales can be maximized. The asset turnover ratio in 2006 is 1.18 times which implies that the BAJAJ AUTO LTD. is producing Rs. 1.18 of sales for one rupee of capital employed in net assets. Compared to the other sequential financial year this ratio is fluctuating. In 2007 its 0.28

and 2008 its 2.95 times it shows sales is increased in year by year. Because of the high investment in the Net assets (new technology) in the year of the 2007 there is the low assets turn over.

RONA i.e. (EBIT(1-T)/NA) increased from 98.9% to 99.3%, and in the year 2008 its decreased from 99.3% to 60.5%. RONA is fluctuation is due to increased in asset turnover ratio and fluctuation in profit margin.

An company can convert its RONA into an impressive ROE through financial efficiency. Financial leverage and debt-equity ratio affects ROE and reflect financial efficiency. ROE is thus a product of a RONA (reflecting operating efficiency) and the financial leverage ratio (reflecting financial efficiency).

The ROE for 2006 is 23.09% which is fluctuating in the year 2007 and 2008 approx 22.37% and 47.62%. The average is thus maintained at nearly 31.29%. In the year 2008 ROE is 47.62% where as the RONA is 60.50%. The company is not able to convert its RONA into an impressive ROE in the years of 2006 and 2007. Whereas in the year of 2008, thought the RONA is decreased to 60.5% the ROE is increased to 22.37% to 47.62% which is higher conversion than the previous years. Here the payment of interest is affected to the profit, it means high borrowing is there in company. The interest as shown in the annual reports of the bajaj auto ltd are in the year 2006 Rs.3.4 crores, 2007 Rs.53.4 crores and in the 2008 Rs.51.6 crores

RETURN ON INVESTMENT:

The term may refer to the total assets or net assets. The fund employed in the net assets is known as a capital employed. Net assets equal net fixed assets plus current assets minus current liability.

ROI before tax

ROI=ROTA= PBIT/ TOTAL ASSETS

ROI=RONA= PBIT/ NET ASSETS

In our automobile two-wheeler industry the ROI (RONA, ROTA) is mentioned in the following table

Table : 4

PERTICULARS	ROTA	RONA
2006	17.42%	98.90 %
2007	17.18%	99.30%
2008	25.95%	60.50%

Graph : 7

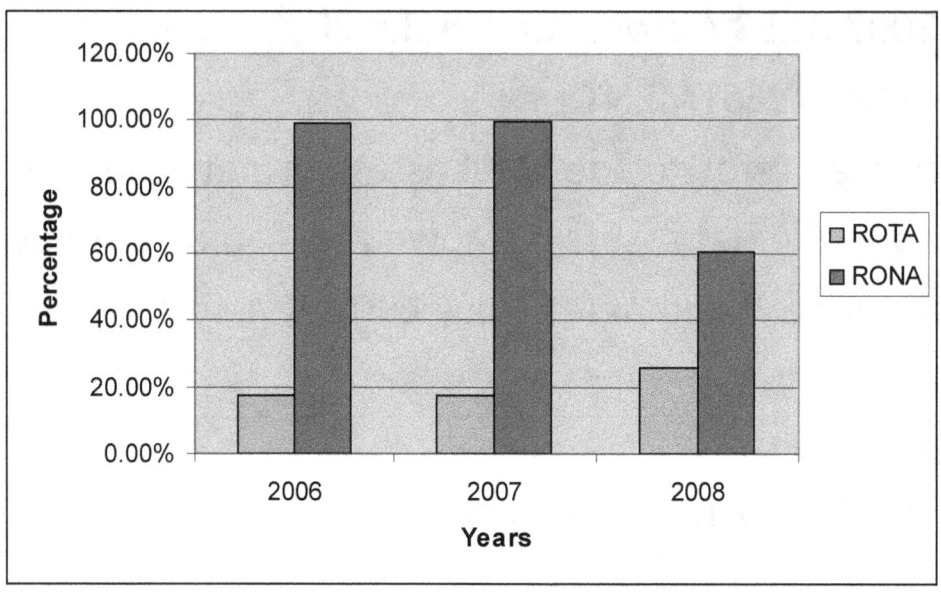

From the above graph and table we have found that the return on assets is increased in the year 2006 and 2007. but it is decreased to 60.5% in 2008, the ROTA is continuous fluctuating because of increasing in total assets and increasing in PBIT that why ROTA is increased and the average of ROTA of the automobile two-wheeler industry is 20.18% it show good position in the economy.

RONA is also increased from sequential years like 2006 its 98.90% ,2007 its 99.30% and 2008 its decreased to 60.50% because of decrease in profit margin thought there is a increase in the asset turnover Ratio.

- **<u>Leverage Analysis</u>**

1) Degree of Operating Leverage: -

Degree of operating leverage is defined as a focus on the

percentage change in earning before interest and taxes relative to a given taxes.

DOL= Contribution/PBIT

Graph ; 8

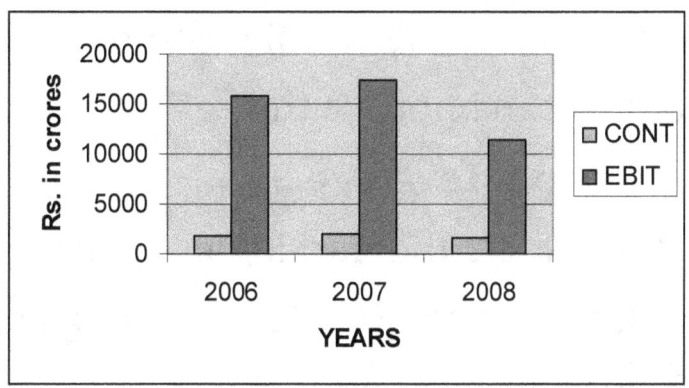

In our Bajaj Auto Ltd. the degree of operating leverage is mentioned in the following table

Table : 5

Particular	2006	2007	2008
DOL	0.1159	0.1179	0.1447

Graph : 9

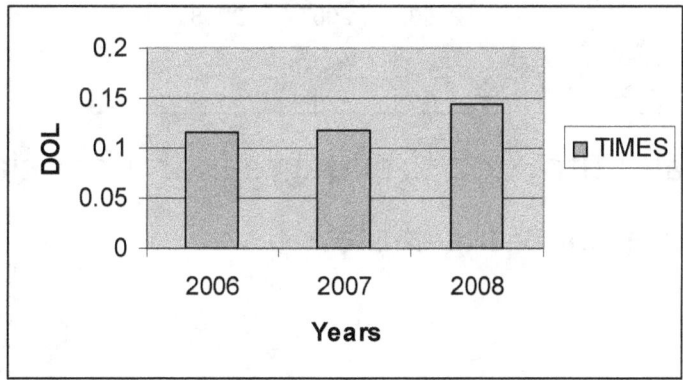

From the above table the DOL is in the year 06 is .1159, its continuous decreased which is in the year 06 is 01179, and in the year 08 its 0.1447, the DOL of 0.11 implies that for a given change in Bajaj Auto Ltd. company sales, PBIT will change by 0.11 times. It is an average position but it is not an worst position of company, if the whole company reduced their variable cost so they can improve this ratio.

2) Degree of Financial Leverage :-

Financial leverage affects the earning per share. The DFL focus on the percentage change in EPS due to given percentage change in EBIT, another method is that it is a ratio of PBIT and PBT (Profit Before Tax).

DFL= PBIT/PBT

Graph : 10

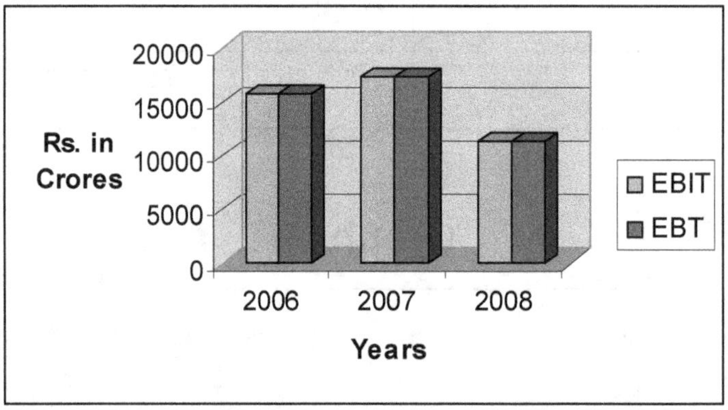

In our Bajaj Auto Co. the degree of financial leverage is mentioned in the following table:-

Table : 6

Particular	2006	2007	2008
DFL	1.003	1.017	1.013

Graph : 11

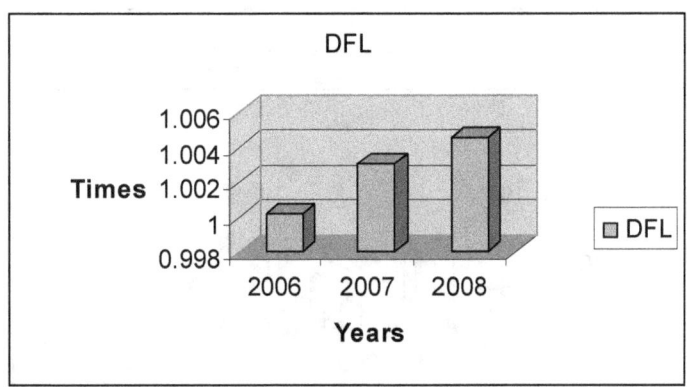

It is observed from the table and from the chart that the overall Bajaj Auto Co. DFL is increased in the Year of 2007, If the economic condition is good and the firms PBIT increasing, its EPS increased faster with the more debt in the capital structure. Here we show the DFL is in the year 07 is 1.017 times it means the company having working in a healthy environment because the company have equal level of debt proportion.

3) Degree of Combined leverage :-

DCL is the product of DOL and DFL. It means the degree of operating leverage and financial leverage can be combined to see the effect of the total leverage on EPS associated with the change in sales.

DCL=DOL*DFL

In our Bajaj Auto Co. the degree of combined leverage is mentioned in the following table:-

Table : 7

Particular	2006	2007	2008
DCL	0.1152	0.1183	0.1453

Graph : 12

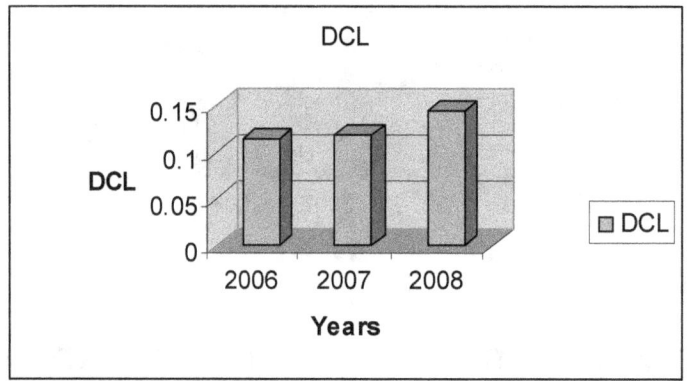

The graph and the table shows that the DCL is gradually reduced from the year 2006 to 2008. The average DCL of the company is 0.1263 times which represents that EPS in the year of 2008 is 54.17 Rs.

Highlights for 2007-08: Bajaj Auto stand-alone

Net sales (net of excise duty) decreased by 6.8% to Rs.86.63 billion. exports increased by 20.8% to Rs.20.48 billion.

Motorcycle sales by volume was 2. 4 million in 2007-08—a fall of 0% over the previous year, versus overall market decline of 7.8%. thus, Bajaj Auto's market share in motorcycles fell marginally from 33.5% in 2006-07 to 32.7% in 2007-08.

Operating profit before tax (PBt) fell by 6.7% — from Rs. 2. 5 billion in 2006-07 to Rs. 0. 2 billion in 2007-08.

Operating working capital

Bajaj Auto enjoys negative working capital. This is even after monies being locked up on account of refunds of VAT and excise duty, amounting to Rs. ,7 0 million.

Table : 8

Rs. In Million	As at 31st March 2008
Current assets	
Inventories	3,496
Sundry debtors	2,753
Cash and bank balances	561
Other current assets	4,438
Sub-total	11,248
Less: Current liabilities	
Sundry creditors	9,445
Advance against orders	948
Other current liabilities	1,032
Sub-total	11,425
Working capital	**-177**

RETURN ON OPERATING CAPITAL EMPLOYED

Table : 9

Rs. In Million	As at 31st March 2008
Fixed assets	12,928
Capital Advances	831
Technical know-how	105
Working capital	-177
Total	**13,687**
Operating profit before interest and taxation	10,172
Pre-tax return on operating capital employed	**74%**

Table no. shows that the operating profit before interest and tax is 10,172 Million and the Pre-Tax Return on Capital Employed is of 74%

HUMAN RESOURCE DEPARTMENT

Recruitment Policy

Bajaj Auto is an equal opportunity employer. Selection is based strictly on individual merit.

A large number of our recruits are fresh engineers and MBAs. Natural attrition is usually taken care of by promotions and horizontal movements within the organization to provide career opportunities for our employees. Occasionally, specific skill-sets may warrant lateral recruitment.

Entry level Recruitment Engineers: We recruit Engineering Graduates from   reputed institutes from all over India. Bajaj Auto enjoys an excellent reputation with all National Institutes of Technology (NITs) and is among the preferred employers for on-campus recruitment. The selection process comprises a written test in technical, analytical and logical reasoning, group discussion and personal interview.

Management Graduates: We recruit management graduates from reputed management institutes all over India. The selection procedure comprises a written test in analytical and logical reasoning, group discussion and personal interview.

All entry-level selections are made through on-campus recruitment only.

After recruitment, new entrants undergo a thorough induction-training programme before their placement in the company. Departments are allocated on the basis of the individual recruit's aptitude and our requirements. Usually, after completing two years of service they are provided opportunities for job rotation.

Work Culture

Our work culture supports and enhances our brand. The Bajaj brand signifies excitement. Bajaj strives to inspire confidence through excitement engineering. The culture is built on core values of learning, innovation, perfection, speed and transparency. Facilitative leadership style helps in developing leaders at all levels and establishes accountability.

Our Brand Values

We live our brand by its values of Innovation, Perfection, and Speed.

Bajaj will be distinctly ahead through excitement engineering.

Innovation is how we create the future. It is a value that provokes us to reach beyond the obvious in pursuit of that which exceeds the ordinary.

Perfection is how we set new standards. It is a value that exhibits our determination to excel by endeavoring to establish new benchmarks all the time.

Speed is how we convey clear conviction. It is a value that keeps us sharply responsive, mirroring our commitment towards our goals and processes.

Competency Building

Bajaj Auto has a very flat organization structure with three management levels. Each level represents a specific role and hence needs relevant competencies. Competency building at Bajaj Auto is a combination of development for current and future roles.

Bajaj auto ltd. cater to these needs by using interventions like development centers, need-based training and job-rotation plans. Bajaj auto ltd. use different methods of imparting training like lectures, group-discussions, role-plays, seminars, outbound training, assignments and on-the-job tasks.

Compensation Philosophy

Bajaj auto ltd. strive to be amongst the top quartile in our compensation structure. Competence and performance are the key drivers of our compensation policy. A significant part of the compensation is in the form of variable pay linked to the individual's and the organization's performance.

People

Rapid changes in systems, processes and the methods of working over the past years have enabled Bajaj Auto achieve a production of 2,723,291 units of vehicles in 2006-07 with the manpower of 10,250- compared to 1.8 million vehicles and 10,914 employees in 2004-05. chart no. highlights how productivity has improved from 116.30 vehicles per employee in 2004-05 to 265.70 vehicles in 2006-07.

The improvement in manpower productivity - measured in terms of vehicles produced per person per year. There has been major improvements since 2003-04: productivity having doubled in four years. This number will further improve in 2007-08 and thereafter, with the Pantnagar unit getting on-stream.

Graph : 13

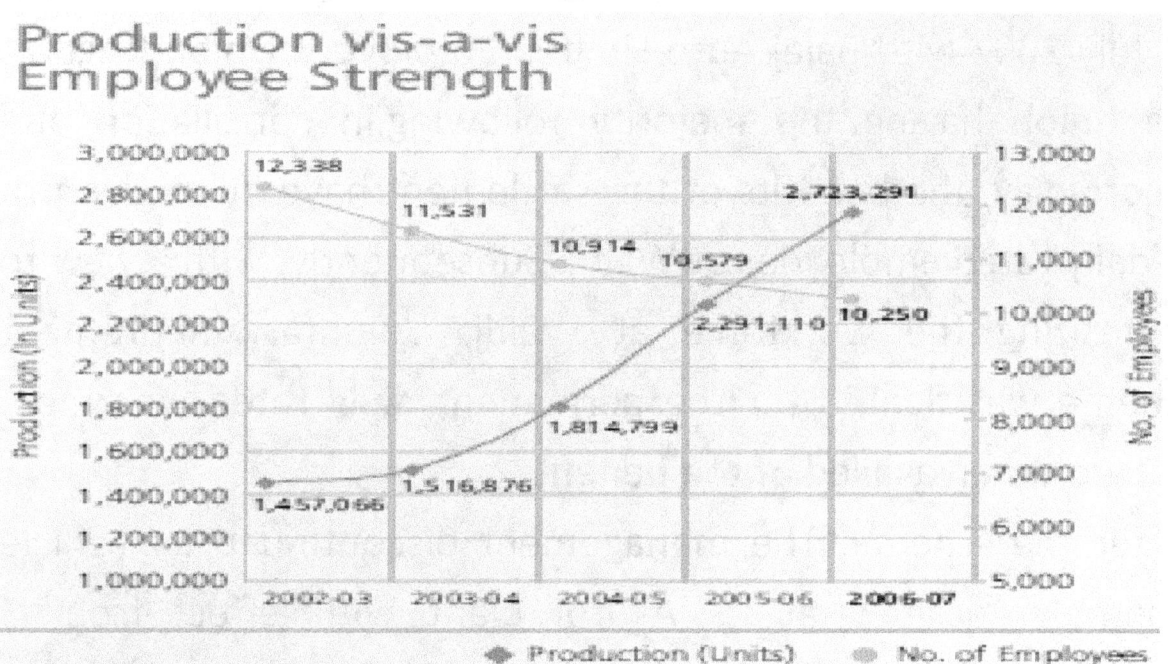

Source: annual report 2006-2007 Bajaj auto ltd

Manpower Productivity

Graph : 14

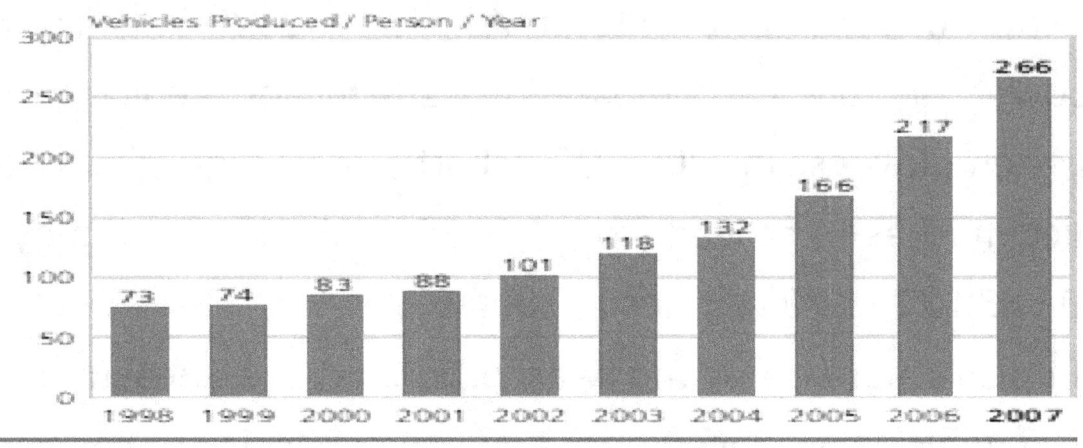

Source – annual report 2006-2007 Bajaj auto ltd.

Industrial Relations

Bharatiya Kamgar Sena(BKS), the recognised union at Waluj, Aurangabad, was de-recognised by Industrial Court on 24 April 2007. Management thereafter signed the wage settlement on 23 July 2007 with Bajaj Auto Limited Employees Union(BALEU), the union having the majority following,in conciliation and accordingly, the benefits of the settlement have been given to all daily rated employees at Waluj. Subsequently, with a view to downsizing the workforce at Waluj, Voluntary Retirement Scheme was floated for the permanent daily rated workmen. 712 workmen availed of the benefit

under the scheme. The management discontinued its vehicle assembly facilities at its Akurdi plant with effect from 3 September 2007 due to the higher cost of manufacturing; as a result of which over 2000 workmen became surplus. Negotiations are on with the newly recognised union viz Vishwa Kalyan Kamgar Sanghatana to find a fair solution. Relations with staff and workmen across the plants at Akurdi, Waluj, Chakan and Pantnagar remained cordial. Government of Maharashtra declared 51 Gunwant Kamgars for the year 2007.

Out of these, Bajaj Auto received 14 awards; 4 workers from Akurdi and 10 from Waluj Plant. Two employees from Waluj Plant have received the prestigious Shram Bhushan and Shram Veer awards this year.

PRODUCTION

Bajaj Auto limited, Waluj, Aurangabad, is a division of Bajaj Auto Limited; Pune a flagship company of Bajaj group was formed by Mr. Jamanalal Bajaj in 1929. Bajaj auto limited, Pune started scooter production in 1960. As an expansion plan, Bajaj Auto Limited, Waluj Plant is started in 1985.

In 1999, a State of Art Plant was started at Chankan. Objectives of Bajaj Auto Limited are to cater the market needs of transportation by providing 2 wheeler and 3 wheeler vehicles. BALW has producing the catalogue products to cater the changing market requirement. Based on the customer feedback, improvements are being made continuously in the existing products. In the process of introducing new products, emission requirements are being taken into consideration and products manufactured are meeting the regulatory requirements.

The site of BAL-W is located in MIDC Waluj area. Bajaj Auto limited is an ISO-9001 company, having ISO-9001(2000) Quality Management certification. A constant watch is kept on the technological development taking place in the areas of energy reduction, waste reduction and pollution prevention. Environment Management System is integral part of overall management system at BAL-W. ISO -14001 certification was awarded to BAL-W in 1997.

Table no- 10

BAJAJ AUTO LIMITED, WALUJ	
Strength - Workmen -	4056 Nos.
Strength - Staff/ Managers -	809 Nos.
Total Plant Area -	600 Acres.
Total Connected Load -	40 MW.
Machines/ Equipments -	3200 Nos.

Modern Machines/ Equipments include
NTC/ Mazak/ Nigatta/ Fortuna/ AMS/Schaudt/HMT
Fanuc Robot drill.
ABB Sweden Robot for Resistance Welding
SAMES Bell Applicator/ Kawasaki Paint Robot.
SMG/ Heilbronn Press.

Source – Annual report 2007 of Bajaj Auto ltd.

In 2006-07, Bajaj Auto limited has posted its highest ever-gross turnover of Rs. 100,761 million and profit after tax at Rs.12, 380 million. Bajaj Auto had sold the 2,399,996 unit of two wheelers in the year of 2006-07. (Chart shown below no.15) Bajaj Auto has resolutely engaged in a process of fundamental changes. This has involved changes in the organizational structure; in product models; in the approach to markets and consumer preferences, in R&D engineering, product design and speed to market; in rationalizing of cost; and in a complete overhaul of the way in which Bajaj Auto do business. This change process is now epitomized by Bajaj Auto's new corporate identity.

Graph : 15.

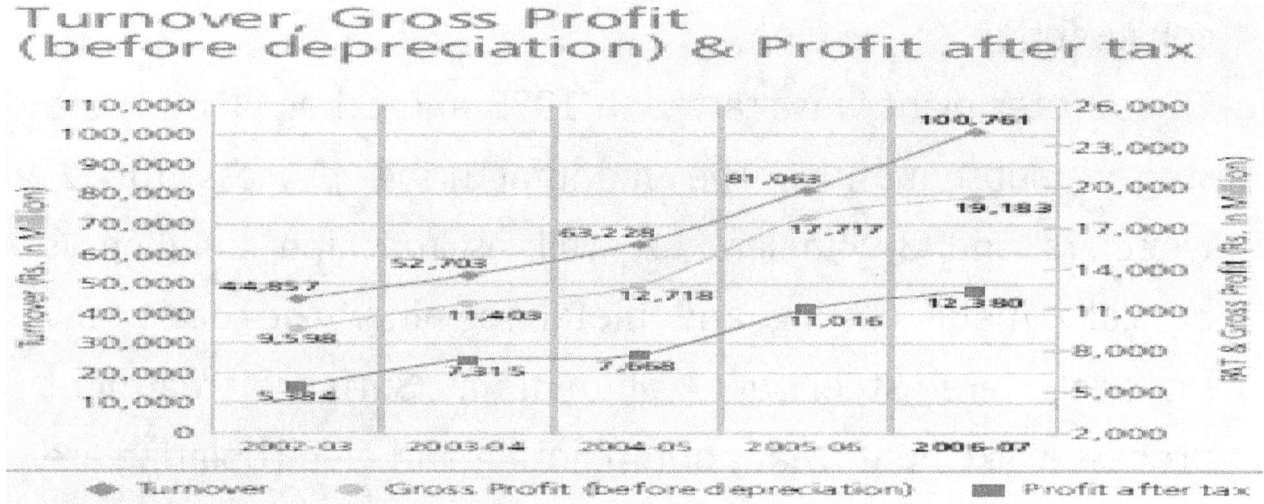

Graph : 16

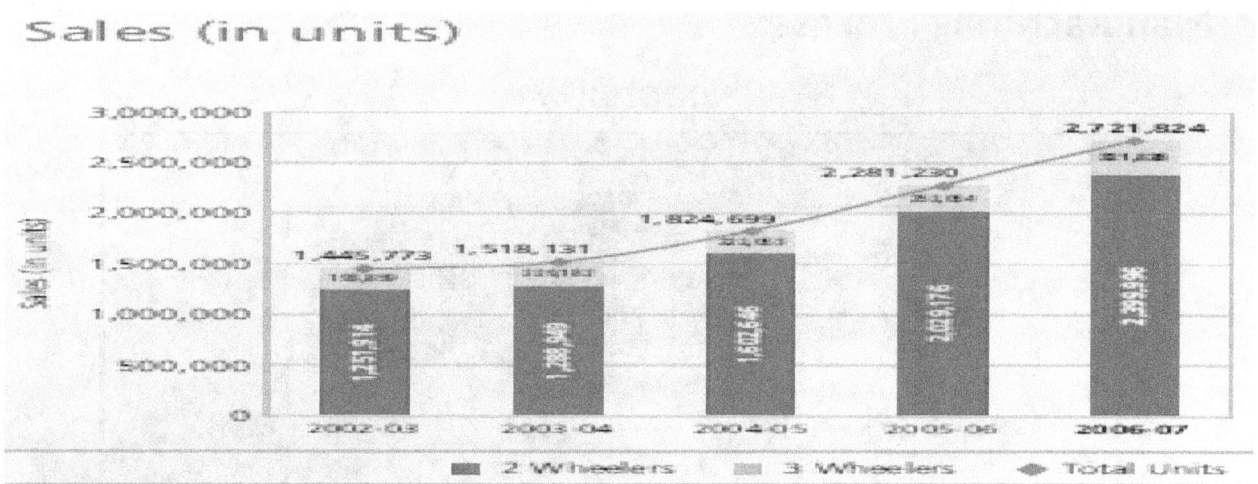

Source for both charts - Bajaj annual report 2006-07

Quality Policy, Environment Policy and TPM Policy are guidelines for our working. Photographs of the same are attached.

Manufacturing Process

The industrial complex of Bajaj Auto Limited-Waluj is spread over an area of 906 acres. The manufacturing activity consists of manufacturing motorized 2-wheelers, 3-wheelers & parts thereof and also machine tools required for captive consumption.

The scooter plant was started in 1985 and other plants were started subsequently. The manufacturing process for 2-wheelers and 3-wheelers as well as machine building is basically metal cutting and metal forming. The basic raw materials are steel and aluminum. Surface treatment processes like heat treatment, painting and electroplating are carried out in the factory.

Manufacturing Process

Graph : 17

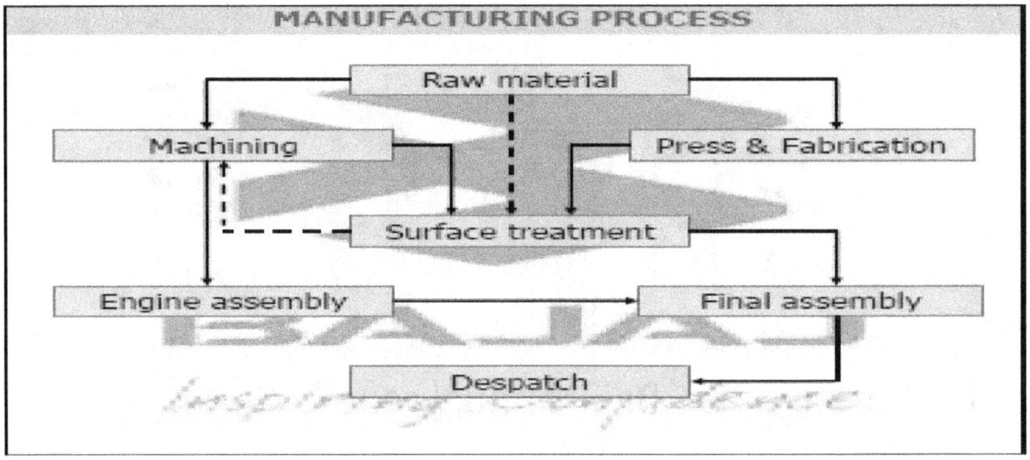

Source:

http://greenbusinesscentre.com/images/Photos/Ene29.pdf

product manufacturing process

Graph : 18

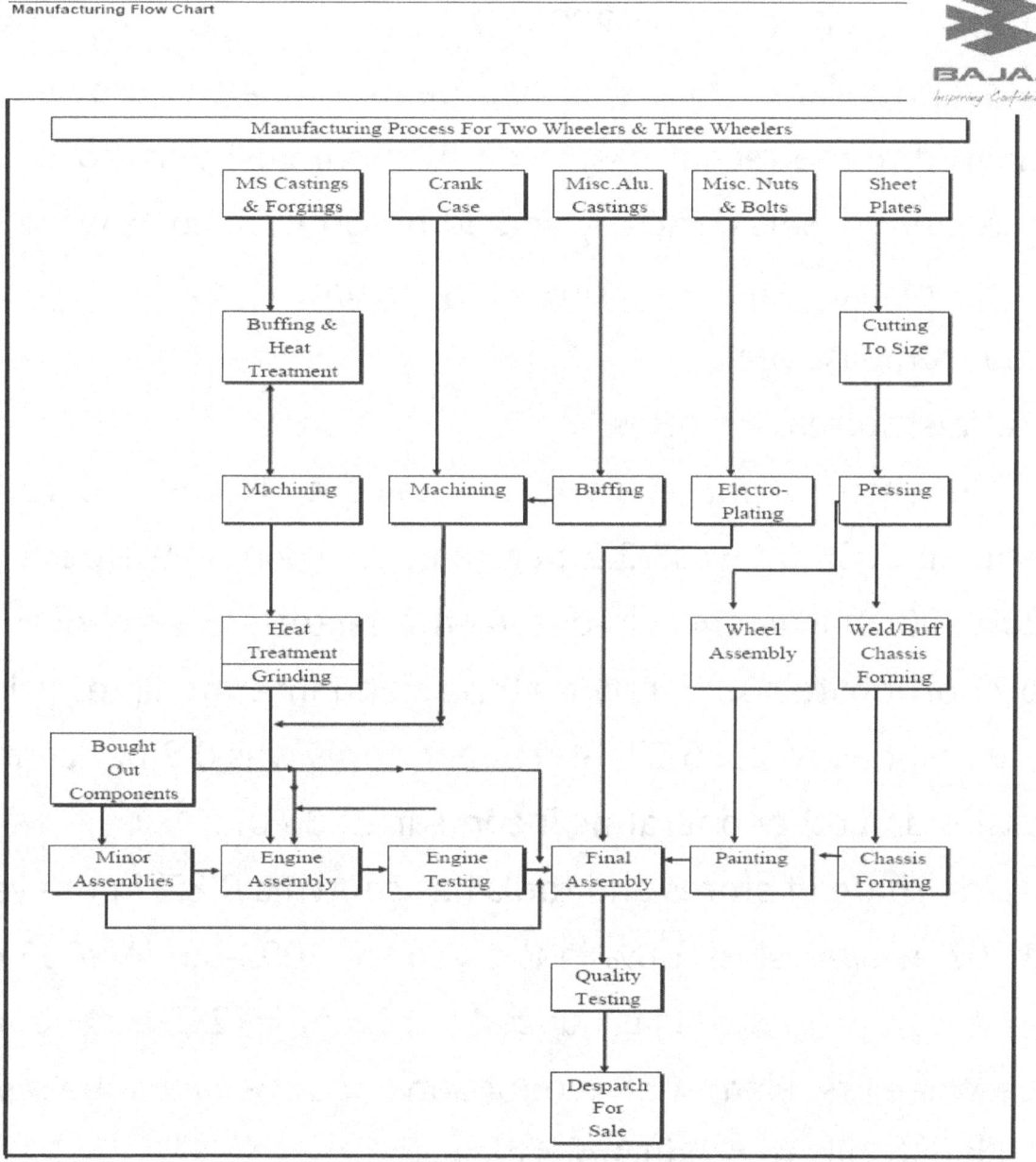

Source: - www.bajajauto.com

Labour, factory and administration costs

Labour costs as a share of sales and other operating income reduced from 3.6 per cent in2005-06 to 3.2 per cent in 2006-07. This has been driven by productivity improvements, which has doubled labour productivity from 132 vehicles per person per year in 2003-04 to 266 in 2006-07 - without a doubling of the wages and salaries bill. This has been a huge improvement compared to the recent past, where labour cost was close to 7 per cent of net sales. Factory and administration costs were 3.4 per cent of sales and other operating income in 2006-07, versus 3.7 per cent last year.

Materials, stores and tools

The share of materials to net sales and other operating income in 2006-07 was 72.2 per cent, as against 69.1 per cent in 2005-06. This is entirely due to the factor stated earlier - a disproportionate rise in raw materials and intermediates prices in the first half of 2006-07. Stores and tools was 0.8 per cent of net sales and other operating income in 2006-07.

The share of stores and tools has shown a 0.8% in the year 2006-07 as against of 1.0% in the year of 2005-06. In 2006-07, Bajaj Auto's three plants produced a total of 2,723,291 two and three-wheelers. Plant wise production capacity shown below in the table. (Units of productions capacity.)

Table : 11.   Plant capacity in Units.

Plant	2006-07	2005-06
Akurdi	720,000	720,000
Waluj	1,860,000	1,500,000
Chakan	960,000	960,000
Pantnagar (new plant)	510,000	—
Total	4,050,000	3,180,000

Source: annual report 2007-08

The pantnagar plant was newly establish in the year of 2006-07 and have the capacity of production of 5,10,000 units. During the year, there was a marginal increase in the capacity at Waluj. The TPM movement in the company's plants continued during the current year and got awarded for their TPM policy. Bajaj Auto started its TPM initiative eight years ago with its manufacturing plants. In March 2007, it achieved a distinct milestone of \having all its manufacturing facilities awarded by JIPM (Japan Institute of Plant Maintenance) as winners of the 'TPM Excellence Category–1'. Thereafter, the Company extended TPM initiatives to all its non manufacturing functions, namely sales, service, engineering, R&D, vendors and dealers.

Last year, TPM at vendor plants received further momentum. 64 vendors received the 'Bajaj Quality Award', compared to 32 in 2006-07. The year also saw five vendors getting the next level of award, the 'Bajaj TPM Award'.

At Chankan, a crankshaft line has been fully automated by the use of nine FUNUC robots. These robots are currently deployed for components loading, unloading from machines, signaling start times, transferring of components from one machine to another, and for the detecting and signaling the state of operation of machines.

This has resulted in elimination components rejections and has also helped to deployed cell members for more value-added activities. World class Manufacturing Plants & State of art Plant at Chakan. World range pf Two-wheelers and Three – wheelers. ISO-9001 (Quality System) and ISO-14001 (Environment system) certification.

The Company remains India's largest exporter of two- and three-wheelers. The total value of exports for 2007-08 was Rs.20.48 billion (Rs.2,048 crore) a 20.8% increase over Rs.16.94 billion (Rs.1,694 crore) in 2006-07, at a time when the rupee appreciated substantially against the US dollar. In terms of volumes, too, Bajaj Auto's international sales achieved an all-time high of 618,341 units of two- and three-wheelers sold during 2007-08, or a growth of 40% over the previous year. Export of two-wheelers increased by 60% to 482,026 units.

Energy Conservation Policy: Method and Working at BAL-W

Top Management Committee fixes Corporate Objective of Energy conservation every year by comparing performance with National / International Benchmarks and targeting for higher achievement. The main objective is to operate most Cost

Effective, Energy Efficient and Environment friendly Plant. Continuous Improvement in Working and also close monitoring is carried out through Energy Management System. Energy audit and efficiency assessment is built-in Quality, Environment and TPM Policy. Awareness of Energy Conservation at all level is reflected in continuous reduction of conversion cost of the vehicles produced year to year.

Method:-

> Technological up gradation - Usage of Flexible Machining Centers instead of Special Purpose Machines.

> Implementation of Streamline Manufacturing Systems. Re-organization of Machines/ Process as per Product Layout.

> Single Digit time in Minutes for Change of Dies/ Tool. Compactness in working area.

> Reduction in rejection less than 1000 PPM (Parts per Million) and aiming for 'ZERO' PPM.

> Nurturing of 'Right First time Ok' culture. Increase in Productivity of the workmen. Improvement in Processes and working methods. Utilization of Idle time. Minimization of Losses by TPM.

> Introduction of Direct on Line of material and elimination of stores.

Graph : 19   Distribution of Electricity.

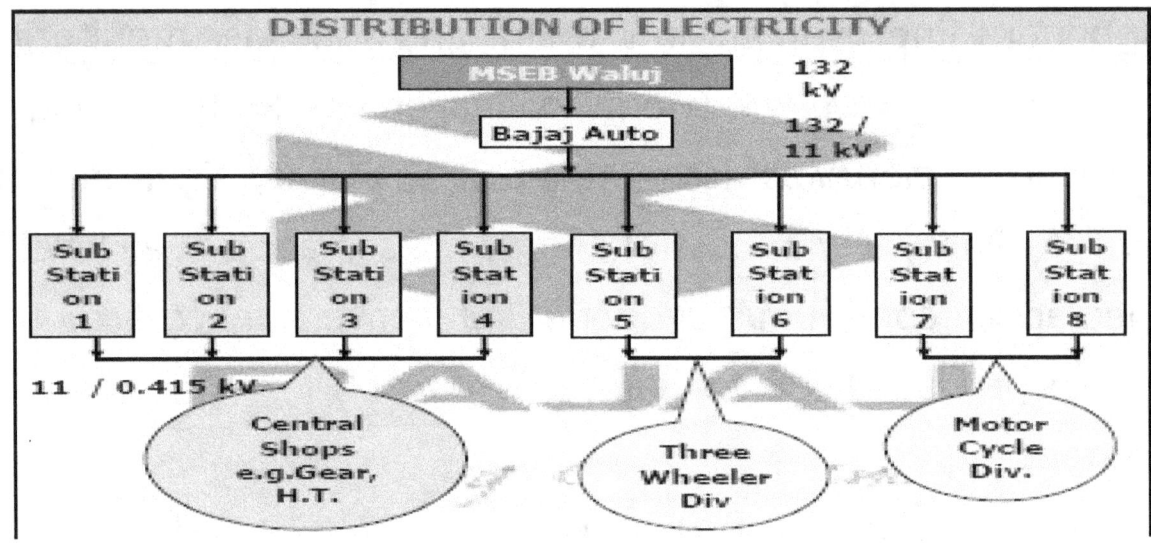

Source :

http://greenbusinesscentre.com/images/Photos/Ene29.pdf

Working :-

Every department sets objectives against environment management plan yearly to conserve Natural resources. Targets are set for Conservation of Natural resources.

Through the systems of Kaizens, TPM Circle/Quality Circles & suggestions, Energy saving proposals are received. Economics & Technical Feasibility is studied by experts for above received proposals for implementation.

Sharing of information through Intra-net among our other plants & horizontal deployment. Awareness level of conservation of energy amongst employee is very high through Training.

The Energy conservation team/cell holds posters competition on Energy & Water Conservation for all employees. This percolates the Energy saving aspects to workmen level. Posters are displayed at work places on awareness of conservation of Energy.

Other policy:-

1. Total Productive maintenance (TPM)

2. Environmental (ISO-14000)

3. Quality (ISO-9000)

Total Productive maintenance (TPM)

"TOTAL PRODUCTIVE MAINTENANCE" as a means of creating a safe and participative work environment in which all employees target the elimination of losses in order to continuously enhance the capacity, flexibility, reliability and capability of its processes, leading to higher employee morale and greater organizational profitability.

Bajaj Auto started its TPM initiative eight years ago with its manufacturing plants. In March 2007, it achieved a distinct milestone of having all its manufacturing facilities awarded by JIPM (Japan Institute of Plant Maintenance) as winners of the 'TPM Excellence Category–1'. Thereafter, the Company extended TPM initiatives to all its non-manufacturing functions, namely sales, service, engineering, R&D, vendors and dealers.

Right from concept planning, various TPM initiatives played key roles in setting up the Company's new green-field plant at Pantnagar. The best kaizens and learning from other plants were implemented from the very first day at Pantnagar. This resulted in rapid ramp-up of production with near zero defects, and the lowest operating cost per vehicle at the plant.

Bajaj Auto initiated TPM in all its 16 vendor plants situated in the Pantnagar vendor cluster. The basic thought was that the plant cannot achieve excellence on its own; and that the vendors and their suppliers needed to be improved simultaneously. The event created history where the mother company with all its vendors doing a concurrent TPM Kick-Off. Conducting TPM on such a scale is definitely a first in India, and possibly in the world.

During 2007-08, other Bajaj Auto plants at Chakan and Waluj (three-wheeler and motorcycles), which had received the TPM Excellence Award in 2006-07, started gearing up for next level of TPM award, namely the 'Special Award for TPM Achievements'. All the three plants — Chakan, Waluj and Pantnagar — will be in a position to apply for this award in 2008-09.

Last year, TPM at vendor plants received further momentum. 64 vendors received the 'Bajaj Quality Award', compared to 32 in 2006-07. The year also saw five vendors getting the next level of award, the 'Bajaj TPM Award'.

Environmental Policy (ISO-14000)

Bajaj Auto Ltd., manufacturer of two and three wheeler vehicles is committed to prevention of pollution, continual improvement of our environmental performance and compliance with all applicable environment legislation and regulation. Towards this, we shall strive to :

Create a proactive environment management system that addresses all environmentally significant aspect related to our products and processes, Minimize the generation of waste and conserve resources through better technology and practices, and Promote environmental awareness amongst our employees and motivate them to fulfill our commitments.

Bajaj auto ltd pledge themselves towards creating and preserving a cleaner environment.

Quality policy (ISO-9000)

Bajaj Auto continues to firmly believe in providing the customer "VALUE FOR MONEY, FOR YEARS" through our products and services. This we shall maintain and improve. In our decision making, quality, safety and service will be given as much consideration as productivity, cost and delivery. Quality shall be built into every aspect of our work life and business operation. Quality improvement and customer satisfaction shall be the responsibility of every employee.

TEAM RESPONSIBILITIES

Top Management:

JMD, ED & VPs Engineering, Operations, Material, Marketing & Finance Setting of Objectives & Targets, Allocations of Budgets Review of Results

Middle Management:

GMs, Divisional Heads, Dept. Managers Brainstorming of alternatives, Activity Planning and Execution Periodical Review of Performance and Reporting

Bottom Management:

Dept. Manager / Supervisors & Workmen Implementation, Sustenance of Set Parameters.

MONITORING AND REPORTING SYSTEM

➢ Measuring Instruments are installed at each manufacturing Areas.

➢ Electrical Power consumption for air Compressors & required CFM are monitored on daily basis.

➢ Power, Fuel & Water consumption are reported daily at shop floor/user department.

➢ Detailed Energy index reported division wise for necessary corrective actions on monthly basis.

> ➤ Cross Functional Team Meetings are conducted weekly for monitoring productivity, Quality & Energy reduction plans to review progress and sharing of thoughts.

> ➤ Cell cost meetings are conducted monthly to monitor cell wise expenses like Tools, Energy & Consumables. Water consumption reviewed Monthly for planning further improvements and monitoring existing plans.

> ➤ Conducting Audit for Air leakage/Water leakage and Immediate Preventive actions.

> ➤ Annual reports of Energy saving generated to set goals for next year.

DISTRIBUTION & LOGISTIC

SUPPLY CHAIN

For Bajaj Auto, the supply chain encompasses the process from vendors to the final customers via manufacturing. Therefore, the Company's supply chain involves as much the vendors and the procurement-to-payment logistics, as it does the manufacturing to selling process, or the order to cash system. Given below are some of the key supply chain initiatives of Bajaj Auto.

The basic distribution channel prevailing includes 3 major steps, like

> Manufacturer: who has the finished products with him.

> State Wise authorized dealers: the manufacturers on certain conditions and criteria's appoint State-wise Authorized Dealers.

> Customers: The customer then can buy the product from the Dealers.

Graph : 20

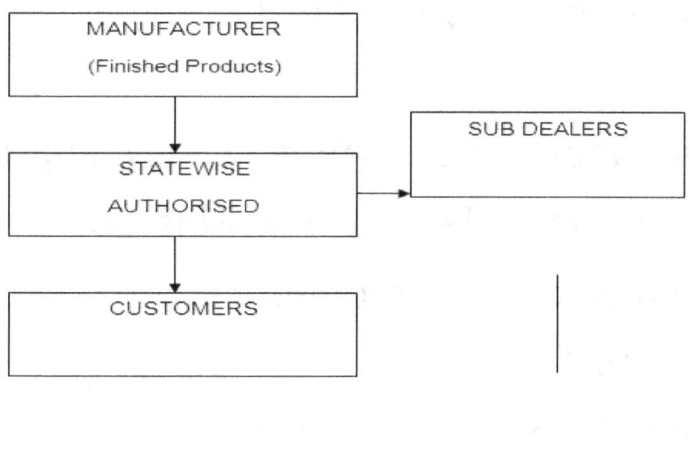

Venders

Most of the Company's vendor initiatives, including the Pantnagar operations and TPM. What needs to be emphasized is that the 16 vendors clustered within the campus of Bajaj Auto's Pantnagar plant were a part of a planned process of project development – where the vendors were fully integrated with the plant, starting with basic raw materials, automated paint, plating and powder coating plants. This has ensured that the maximum possible value addition is done within Uttarakhand, so as to maximize the tax advantage and make Bajaj Auto's motorcycles even more cost competitive. Initial facilities created by vendors at Pantnagar at an aggregate investment of Rs.5 billion (Rs.500 crore) are for half million motorcycles per year, which will be increased with balancing investments to produce one million motorcycles per year to synchronize with the Company's plans.

Dealers

Bajaj Auto has adopted a channel policy approach which is unique in the automobile industry. This policy and its linked initiatives are guided by the requirements of specific sets of the Company's final customers.

1. The Primary Channel: This comprises 408 exclusive two-wheeler dealers, 75 exclusive three-wheeler dealers, and 98 dealers who deal in both product categories. Bajaj Auto has followed a policy of systematic network consolidation, in which the primary dealerships have been given a larger scale and scope to operate based on their strengths.

2. The Secondary Channel: Much of Bajaj Auto's recent success can be attributed to policy of rapidly adding to the number of secondary outlets, which provide sales, service and spares support in the vast hinterland of India. These are in the form of 1,500 Authorized Service Centers (ASC), 4,500 Rural Service Outlets (RSO), and 750 Young Engineer Service (YES) centers in the towns and cities.

3. The Rural India Foray : The Company has been aggressively pursuing initiatives to increase two-wheeler penetration in rural India. A large number of rural outlets were added to the

network during the year, which not only increased hinterland sales but also gave additional employment in the rural sector.

4. Pro-biking: This initiative sits far away from the rural India play but is no less important. Bajaj Auto believes that young India doesn't pay to buy motorcycles; it pays to buy excitement and exhilaration. The Pro-biking initiative, which was kicked off with the inauguration of first store in Pune in August 2005, aims precisely at creating this thrill. Owned and operated by Bajaj Auto, Pro-biking showrooms are now operational in Mumbai, Kolkatta, Chennai, Hyderabad and Ahmedabad.

RESEARCH & DEVELOPMENT

Research & development and technology absorption

The company's R & D efforts during the year remained focused on:

> Introduction of new products.

> Upgrading of current products for improved performance and reliability.

> Launching of variants in the current products for meeting specific customer needs.

> Developments in engine and vehicle aggregates to meet new motor vehicle regulations and tightening emission norms.

During 2007-08, Bajaj Auto's R&D was primarily involved with the work on the next wave of products to be launched in 2008-09. Two important products which demonstrated the Company's technological prowess were also launched during the year — the XCD 125 DTS -Si and the Three-wheeler Direct Injected auto rickshaw.

R&D was primarily involved with the work on the next wave of products to be launched in the year 2008-09. Two important products which demonstrated the technical prowess of the company were launched during 2008. These were the XCD 125 cc DTS-Si and the Three-wheeler Direct Injected auto rickshaw.

Company continues to build its research and development infrastructure in all the areas of design, prototyping and validation. These are long term investments and are aimed to give flexibility, speed and insight into every field of interest in creating the product. The expenditure on research and development during 2007-08 and in the previous year was:

Table : 12 Investment pattern of Bajaj Auto Ltd.

	2007-08 Rs. In Million	2006-07 * Rs. In Million
i. Capital (including technical know-how)	481.4	473.4
ii. Recurring	706.0	676.9
	1,187.4	1,150.3
iii. Total research and development expenditure as a percentage of sales, net of excise duty	1.37	1.24

* Figures pertain to the erstwhile Bajaj Auto Ltd.

Source: Annual report 2007-08

BAL to improve on new launches

XCD 125 DTS-Si

The XCD 125 DTS-Si has been touched upon earlier. The platform is strategically important, as it uses technological differentiation to increase the penetration of Bajaj Auto's motorcycles in the large 125 cc segment. The XCD 125 DTS -Si is the result of the cumulative experience of many years of engine and vehicle development in Bajaj Auto. DTS –Si represents the latest advancements in modifying the Company's patented DTS -i technology to further enhance the combustion by incorporating a swirl motion in the combustion chamber. The combustion is controlled by using an advanced microcontroller-based ECU, which gives both ignition and fuel controls based on inputs of load, revolutions per minute and temperature. The engine cuts down weight and friction to match numbers of a typical 100cc engine. The XCD 125 DTS -Si has been engineered to cut down weight, while having on board advanced features like LCD speedometer, LED tail lamps and tank spoilers.

Better value:

Earlier, people were willing to pay a premium for Hero Honda products because of its brand image and perceived technological superiority, which was why a product such as the caliber, in spite of being a technologically better product, did not get as much success against the Splendor when priced at same level. But now with the tremendous success of its DTS-Si technology, customers perceived value in BAL's competitively priced products.

Bajaj Auto has a huge, extensive and very well-equipped Research and Development wing geared to meet two critical organizational goals: development of exciting new products that anticipate and meet emerging customer needs in India and abroad, and development of eco-friendly automobile technologies.

While the manpower strength of the R&D represents a cross-section of in-depth design and engineering expertise, the company has also been investing heavily in the latest, sophisticated technologies to scale down product development lifecycles and enhance testing capabilities.

Bajaj Auto R&D also enjoys access to the specialized expertise of leading international design and automobile engineering companies working in specific areas.

Based on their own brand of globalization, they have built their distribution network over 60 countries worldwide and multiplied the exports from 1% of total turnover in Fiscal 1989-90 to over 5% in Fiscal 1996-97.

The countries where their products have a large market are USA, Argentina, Colombia, Peru, Bangladesh, Sri Lanka, Italy,

Sweden, Germany, Iran and Egypt. Bajaj leads Colombia with 65% of the scooter market, in Uruguay with 30% of the motorcycle market and in Bangladesh with 95% of the three-wheeler market.

Several new models are being developed specifically for global markets and with these the company will progressively endeavor to establish its presence in Europe too.

FIVE FORCE MODEL

Entry Barriers:

Entry barriers are high.

- The market runs on high economies of scale and on high economies of scope.
- The need for technical expertise is high.
- Owning a strong distribution network is important and is very costly.

All these make the barrier high enough to be a deterrent for new entrants.

Supplier Bargaining Power:

Suppliers of auto components are fragmented and are extremely critical for this industry since most of the component work is outsourced. Proper supply chain management is a costly yet critical need.

Buyer's Bargaining Power:

Buyers in automobile market have more choice to choose from and the increasing competition is driving the bargaining power of customers uphill. With more models to choose from in almost all categories, the market forces have empowered the buyers to a large extent.

Industry Rivalry:

The industry rivalry is extremely high with any product being matched in a few months by competitor. This instinct of the industry is primarily driven by the technical capabilities acquired over years of gestation under the technical collaboration with international players.

Substitutes:

There is no perfect substitute to this industry. Also, if there is any substitute to a two-wheeler, Bajaj has presence in it. Cars, which again are a mode of transport, do never directly compete or come in consideration while selecting a two-wheeler, cycles do never even compete with the low entry level moped for even this choice comes at a comparatively higher economic potential.

KEY EARNING FACTORS

Below are the key factors, which strongly affect the auto industry: -

Government policy impact on petrol prices: Petrol prices determine the running cost of two/three wheelers expressed in Rupees per kilometer.

Petrol prices are the highest in India as GOI subsidizes kerosene and diesel. But with the recent change in GOI policy to reduce the subsidy, the prices of petrol will remain constant at the current prices. This will have a positive effect on purchases of two/three wheelers.

Improvement in disposable income: With the increase in salary levels, due to entry of multinationals following liberalization process and fifth pay commission, the disposable income has improved exponentially over the years. This will have multiplier effect on demand for consumer durables including two-wheelers.

Changes in prices of second-hand cars: The second hand car prices of small cars have come down sharply in the recent past. This will shift the demand from higher-end two-wheelers to cars and affect the demand for two-wheelers negatively. A further drop in second-hand car prices will lead to pressure on the two-wheeler majors who plan to release higher-end scooters and motorcycles.

Implementation of mass transport system: Many states have planned to implement mass transport systems in state capitals in the future. This will have negative impact on demand for two-wheelers in the long run. But taking into account the delays involved in implementation of such large infrastructure projects the demand to be affected only five to seven years down the line.

Availability of credit for vehicle purchase: The availability and cost of finance affects the demand for two- and three-wheelers as the trend for increased credit purchases for consumer durables have increased over the years. Therefore, any change with respect to any of these two parameters as a result of change in RBI policy has to be closely watched to assess the demand for two- and three-wheelers

SWOT Analysis

Let's analyze the position of Bajaj in the current market set-up, evaluating its strengths, weaknesses, threats and opportunities available.

Strengths:

> ➤ Bajaj is a well-established Brand name in the scooter segment.
> ➤ Bajaj has highly experienced management.
> ➤ Product design and development capabilities.
> ➤ Extensive R & D focus.
> ➤ Widespread distribution network.
> ➤ High performance products across all categories.

➢ High export to domestic sales ratio.

➢ Great financial support network (For financing the automobile)

➢ High economies of scale.

➢ High economies of scope.

Weaknesses:

➢ Hasn't employed the excess cash for long.

➢ Still has no established brand to match Hero Honda's Splendor in commuter segment.

➢ Not a global player in spite of huge volumes.

➢ Not a globally recognizable brand (unlike the JV partner Kawasaki)

Opportunities:

➢ Double-digit growth in two-wheeler market.

➢ Untapped market above 180 cc in motorcycles.

➢ More maturity and movement towards higher-end motorcycles.

➢ The growing gearless trendy scooters and scooterette market.

➢ Growing world demand for entry-level motorcycles especially in emerging markets.

➢ Scope of entering in to the low cost four wheelers. (Source :-Business Standard : June 18,2008) (Bajaj Auto prepares to enter India Small car Market. Source: forbes.com, January 8,2008)

Threats:

> The competition catches-up any new innovation in no time.

> Threat of cheap imported motorcycles from China.

> Margins getting squeezed from both the directions (Price as well as Cost)

> TATA Ace is a serious competition for the three-wheeler cargo segment.

FUTURE OUTLOOKS

Although the avalanche of motorcycles offered Indian consumers a wide variety of models to choose from, it also resulted in increased pressure on the companies to concentrate on cost-cuts, technology enhancements and up-gradations and styling. Their margins came under pressure as marketing costs escalated.

The companies were forced to reduce prices and offer discounts to survive the competition. Moreover, analysts were skeptical about the segment's ability to maintain the growth rate in the years to come. One of the major assumptions underlying the motorcycles rush was that if the market was considerably large and was growing at a constant pace, there was room for a profitable existence for all brands.

In 2001, there were over 30 motorcycle brands in the market. However, with the top five brands accounting for more than 60% of the market, only 40% of the market was available for all other new brands put together. Despite the launch of more vehicles, the survival prospects of many of the individual brands were deemed to be rather bleak.

Further, the growth in the motorcycle segment was dependant on continuing favorable market conditions. Analysts claimed that to sustain this growth rate, the segment would have to completely cannibalize the market for scooters and a considerable part of the market for scooterettes and mopeds.

Considering the fast growing scooterettes segment, with high demand from female customers, followed by the moderately growing moped segment and the restructuring in the scooter segment with major national and foreign players reinforcing their presence, it was unlikely that the entire growth in the two-wheeler sector would be due to motorcycles.

Analysts also commented that as the two-wheeler industry had grown steadily for eight years, stages in the product life cycle would apply to the field sooner, rather than later and the decline stage would invariably come some day. There was little differentiation between the brands being launched apart from styling as most companies had introduced their four-stroke vehicles.

With the failure of the joint ventures, the expected introduction of cheaper Chinese brands, stringent emission norms and threat from major international players, the survival of indigenous brands looked uncertain. Constrained with the ruling price levels in the market place, limited infrastructure and lack of technological innovations when compared to their foreign counterparts, whether the Indian companies would succeed in generating the kind of volumes needed to sustain in the competitive motorcycle market, remains to be seen.

CONCLUSION & SUGGESSION

CONCLUSIONS :

- ➢ Bajaj is currently India's largest two wheeler manufacturers and one of the biggest in the world.
- ➢ Bajaj Auto Ltd's motorcycle and two wheeler market share in 2007 was 33.5% and in 2008 it was 30.8%.
- ➢ The company has a good presence in the premium bike segment with it's pulsar and Eliminator models.
- ➢ Bajaj auto will also launch small size car with low cost in Indian market.
- ➢ It is doing well in the entry-level segment with it's Boxer, CT-100, the modified version of Boxer too has done well for the company.
- ➢ However, Hero Honda dominates the executive segment, which is the highest selling segment in motorcycle, with

42% market share. Bajaj auto holds 27% market share in same segment.

➢ In the past, Hero Honda defeated Bajaj auto in two wheelers with just one fuel-efficient bike. Honda Motor corporation, Japan is planning something similar through it's subsidiary, HMSI, HMSI has already gained a large chunk of Bajaj auto's share in scooters, especially with its ungeared range of scooters, overtaking Bajaj Auto ltd as the leading scooter manufacturer.

➢ Bajaj Ltd sales of two wheeler in 2007 was 8.47 million while in 2008 it was 8.07 million.

➢ Export of Bajaj auto ltd was growing by 60 % with total export of two wheeler in 2007 was 300656 and in 2008 it was 481,549.

➢ Bajaj is taking classical marketing route to enter the rural mind space.

SUGGESTIONS :

Focus on High Margin Products: Around 50% of the two-wheeler consumers buy high quality products (products of executive and premium segment motorcycles). Margins on these products are higher.

BAL should adopt a deliberate strategy of focusing on executive and premium segment motorcycles and three-wheelers, and is reducing its dependence on lower-end of motorcycles and scooters segment.

High margin products - Pulsar, Discover, Three-wheelers, Avenger.

Low margin products - Platina, Scooters, Mopeds.

Now with increasing competition in the economy segment and limited scope from cost saving measures, it is believed this strategy of focusing on higher margin products would enable the company in retaining its operating margins.

Below are other useful recommendations: -

- Company should keep focusing on the fast growing motorcycle segment.

- In view of the new threat posed by Honda Motors in the scooter segment, the company needs to review its products line-up and launch new products to cater the changed demand.

- The company needs to take a look at its ungeared scooters offerings and need to adapt to the latest trends.

- The company needs to tap the export market more efficiently as there is a huge potential to make India as the world's two-wheelers production base. For this, it needs to look for joint ventures abroad.

- It needs to target the young age group more effectively as this group is extremely trend savvy. The advertising should have a fresh look and the product should live up to the Gen-X's expectations.

➢ Rural Development, good monsoon should witness a healthy growth in 2006-07.

➢ Because of the recession in the market company's product demand was decrease in 2008.

➢ Fuel Injection on 2 wheeler is round the corner. My educated guess about the Honda bikes in future will be fuel injected, because , Honda has already announced that all its motorcycle or scooters would be fuel injected by 2010 so Bajaj auto ltd should invest in R & D and develop fuel injection 2 wheelers.

➢ Big Manufacturer like Bajaj Auto can arm twist suppliers to deliver parts cheaper, which the suppliers won't mind doing considering the volumes that these offer. Without volumes, one is not in a position to get the best prices and without best component prices, the prices of final product goes up. Fighting with Bajaj auto will require reduction in the selling price of the bikes thus decreasing the profit margins.

➢ This is like the vicious circle : low volumes > high component prices > high final price > still lower volumes > low profitability or another way forward may be low volumes > high component prices > low final prices > compromise on margins > low profitability.

➢ The only way out seems to be technical innovation which can give a low volumes company advantage over a high volume one. Unfortunately low volumes > low profitability also means that less investment in R & D. or in some cases, where R&D does get a priority, it is mostly copied very quickly by rivals as most of the R & d is supplier driven.

BIBLIOGRAPHY

MAGAZINES

- Business Today published by India today Grouped
- Business world, January ,2009.
- Auto India December, 2008.

www.ingramcontent.com/pod-product-compliance
Lightning Source LLC
Chambersburg PA
CBHW080830180526
45168CB00006B/2640